THE MIRRORS OF DOWNING STREET

RT. HON. DAVID LLOYD GEORGE

THE MIRRORS OF DOWNING STREET

SOME POLITICAL REFLECTIONS

BY

A GENTLEMAN WITH A DUSTER

Begbie

"Right and wrong are in the nature of things. They are not words and phrases. They are in the nature of things, and if you transgress the laws laid down, imposed by the nature of things, depend upon it you will pay the penalty."

JOHN MORLEY.

ILLUSTRATED

G. P. PUTNAM'S SONS
NEW YORK AND LONDON
The Knickerbocker Press
1921

Printed in the United States of America

PUBLISHERS' NOTE

AMERICA and England have worked and fought together and have brought to a successful conclusion
the great war in defence of civilization against a military imperialism which was threatening to dominate
the world. They have now responsibilities together in
connection with the measures needed to assure the
continued peace of the world and to secure, particularly
for the smaller states and for communities not in a
position to become independent nations, the protection
of their liberties, to which they have as assured a right
as that asserted by a state of first importance which
can support its claims with great armies.

In this work of helping to adjust the present urgent
problems of the world, England is demanding co-oper-
ation from America. America could not if she would,
and would not if she could, escape her responsibilities,
as the strongest nation in the world, a nation standing
for the rights of men, for leadership in the family of
nations. With these joint responsibilities resting upon
England and America, the personalities of the men
who have during the past few years had in their hands
the direction of the affairs of the United Kingdom and

of the great British Commonwealth must possess an assured interest for every intelligent American.

The clever author of *The Mirrors of Downing Street* has brought together a series of critical and biographical studies, presented as "reflections" from the mirror in the Imperial council chamber, of thirteen typical Britons who have done noteworthy work during the years of the war and who are now grappling with the problems of the peace. The name of the author is not given, but he is evidently one who has had intimate personal association with the statesmen and administrators whose characters he presents. These analyses are not always sympathetic, and we are not prepared to say that they will be accepted as final. They are, however, based upon full knowledge of the conditions and a close personal study of the men. Intelligent Americans will be interested in the opinions held by a clear-headed, capable English writer of the characters of leaders like Mr. Asquith, Lloyd George, Mr. Balfour, Lord Robert Cecil, Winston Churchill, and others, and they will find in these pages first-hand information and clever and incisive studies of noteworthy men whose influence has counted, and is still to count, in shaping the history of Britain and of the world.

G. H. P.

New York, December, 1920.

INTRODUCTION

LET me say that I hope I have not betrayed any confidences in these sketches.

Public men must expect criticism, and no criticism is so good for them, and therefore for the State, as criticism of character; but their position is difficult, and they may justly complain when those to whom they have spoken in the candour of private conversation make use of such confidences for a public purpose.

If here and there I have in any degree approached this offence, let me urge two excuses. First, inspired by a pure purpose I might very easily have said far more than I have said: and, second, my purpose is neither to grind my own axe (as witness my anonymity) nor to inflict personal pain (as witness my effort to be just in all cases), but truly to raise the tone of our public life.

It is the conviction that the tone of our public life is low, and that this low tone is reacting disastrously in many directions, which has set me about these studies in political personality.

There is too much dust on the mirrors of Downing Street for our public men to see themselves as others see them. Some of that dust is from the war; some of it is the old-fashioned political dust intended for the eyes of the public; but I think that the worst of all hindrances to true vision is breathed on the mirrors by those self-regarding public men in whom principle is crumbling and moral earnestness is beginning to moulder. One would wipe away those smears.

My duster is honest cotton; the hand that holds it is at least clean; and the energy of the rubbing is inspired solely by the hope that such labour may be of some benefit to my country.

I think our statesmen may be better servants of the great nation they have the honour to serve if they see themselves as others see them—others who are not political adversaries, and who are more interested in the moral and intellectual condition of the State than in the fortunes of its parties.

No man can ever be worthy of England; but we must be anxious when the heart and centre of public service are not an earnest desire to be as worthy of her as possible.

CONTENTS

ILLUSTRATIONS

MR. LLOYD GEORGE

THE RT. HON. DAVID LLOYD GEORGE

Born, Manchester, 1863; son of the late Wm. George, Master of the Hope Street Unitarian Schools, Liverpool. Educated in a Welsh Church School and under tutors. By profession a solicitor. President of the Board of Trade, 1905-8; Chancellor of the Exchequer, 1908-15; Minister of Munitions, 1915-16; Secretary for War, 1916; Prime Minister, 1916-20.

CHAPTER I

MR. LLOYD GEORGE

"And wars, like mists that rise against the sun,
Made him but greater seem, not greater grow."

DRYDEN.

IF you think about it, no one since Napoleon has appeared on the earth who attracts so universal an interest as Mr. Lloyd George. This is a rather startling thought.

It is significant, I think, how completely a politician should overshadow all the great soldiers and sailors charged with their nation's very life in the severest and infinitely the most critical military struggle of man's history.

A democratic age, lacking in colour, and antipathetic to romance, somewhat obscures for us the pictorial achievement of this remarkable figure. He lacks only a crown, a robe, and a gilded chair easily to outshine in visible picturesqueness the great Emperor. His achievement, when we consider what hung upon it, is greater than Napoleon's, the narrative of his origin more romantic, his character more complex. And yet who does not feel the greatness of Napoleon?—and who does not suspect the shallowness of Mr. Lloyd George?

History, it is certain, will unmask his pretensions to

3

grandeur with a rough, perhaps with an angry hand; but all the more because of this unmasking posterity will continue to crowd about the exposed hero asking, and perhaps for centuries continuing to ask, questions concerning his place in the history of the world. "How came it, man of straw, that in Armageddon there was none greater than you?"

The coldest-blooded amongst us, Mr. Massingham of *The Nation* for example, must confess that it was a moment rich in the emotion which bestows immortality on incident when this son of a village schoolmaster, who grew up in a shoemaker's shop, and whose boyish games were played in the street of a Welsh hamlet remote from all the refinements of civilization and all the clangours of industrialism, announced to a breathless Europe without any pomposity of phrase and with but a brief and contemptuous gesture of dismissal the passing away from the world's stage of the Hapsburgs and Hohenzollerns —those ancient, long glorious, and most puissant houses whose history for an æon was the history of Europe.

Such topsy-turvydom, such historical anarchy, tilts the figure of Mr. Lloyd George into a salience so conspicuous that for a moment one is tempted to confuse prominence with eminence, and to mistake the slagheap of upheaval for the peaks of Olympus.

But how is it that this politician has attained even to such super-prominence?

Another incident of which the public knows nothing, helps one, I think, to answer this question. Early in the struggle to get munitions for our soldiers a meeting of all the principal manufacturers of armaments was held in Whitehall with the object of persuading them to pool their trade secrets. For a long time this meeting was nothing more than a succession of blunt speeches on the part of provincial manufacturers, showing with an unanswerable commercial logic that the suggestion of revealing these secrets on which their fortunes depended was beyond the bounds of reason. All the interjected arguments of the military and official gentlemen representing the Government were easily proved by these hard-headed manufacturers, responsible to their workpeople and shareholders for the prosperity of their competing undertakings, to be impracticable if not preposterous.

At a moment when the proposal of the Government seemed lost, Mr. Lloyd George leant forward in his chair, very pale, very quiet, and very earnest. "Gentlemen," he said in a voice which produced an extraordinary hush, "have you forgotten that your sons, at this very moment, are being killed—killed in hundreds and thousands? They are being killed by German guns for want of British guns. Your sons, your brothers—boys at the dawn of manhood!—they are being wiped out of life in thousands! Gentlemen, give me guns. Don't think of your trade secrets. Think of your children. Help them! Give me those guns."

This was no stage acting. His voice broke, his eyes filled with tears, and his hand, holding a piece of notepaper before him, shook like a leaf. There was not a man who heard him whose heart was not touched, and whose humanity was not quickened. The trade secrets were pooled. The supply of munitions was hastened.

This is the secret of his power. No man of our period, when he is profoundly moved, and when he permits his genuine emotion to carry him away, can utter *an appeal to conscience* with anything like so compelling a simplicity. His failure lies in a growing tendency to discard an instinctive emotionalism for a calculated astuteness which too often attempts to hide its cunning under the garb of honest sentiment. His intuitions are unrivalled: his reasoning powers inconsiderable.

When Mr. Lloyd George first came to London he shared not only a room in Gray's Inn, but the one bed that garret contained with a fellow-countryman. They were both inconveniently poor, but Mr. Lloyd George the poorer in this, that as a member of Parliament his expenses were greater. The fellow-lodger, who afterwards became private secretary to one of Mr. Lloyd George's rivals, has told me that no public speech of Mr. Lloyd George ever equalled in pathos and power the speeches which the young member of Parliament would often make in those hungry days, seated on the edge of the bed, or pacing to and fro in the room, speeches lit by one passion and directed to one great object, lit by the passion of justice, directed to the liberation of all peoples oppressed by every form of tyranny.

This spirit of the intuitional reformer, who feels

cruelty and wrong like a pain in his own blood, is still present in Mr. Lloyd George, but it is no longer the central passion of his life. It is, rather, an aside: as it were a memory that revives only in leisure hours. On several occasions he has spoken to me of the sorrows and sufferings of humanity with an unmistakable sympathy. I remember in particular one occasion on which he told me the story of his boyhood: it was a moving narrative, for never once did he refer to his own personal deprivations, never once express regret for his own loss of powerful encouragements in the important years of boyhood. The story was the story of his widowed mother and of her heroic struggle, keeping house for her shoemaking brother-in-law on the little money earned by the old bachelor's village cobbling, to save sixpence a week—sixpence to be gratefully returned to him on Saturday night. "That is the life of the poor!" he exclaimed earnestly. Then he added with bitterness, "And when I try to give them five shillings a week in their old age I am called the 'Cad of the Cabinet'!"

Nothing in his life is finer than the struggle he waged with the Liberal Cabinet during his days as Chancellor of the Exchequer. The private opposition he encountered in Downing Street, the hatred and contempt of some of his Liberal colleagues, was exceeded on the other side of politics only in the violent mind of Sir Edward Carson. Even the gentle John Morley was troubled by his hot insistences. "I had better go," he said to Mr. Lloyd George; "I am getting old: I have nothing now for you but criticism." To which the other replied, "Lord Morley, I would sooner have your criticism than the praise of any man living"—a perfectly sincere remark, sincere, I mean, with the emotionalism of the moment. His schemes were disordered and crude; nevertheless the spirit that informed them was like a new birth in the politics of the whole world. A friend of mine told me that he had seen pictures of Mr. Lloyd George on the walls of peasants' houses in the remotest villages of Russia.

But those days have departed and taken with them the fire of Mr. Lloyd George's passion. The laboured peroration about the hills of his ancestors, repeated to the point of the ridiculous, is all now left of that fervid period. He has ceased to be a prophet. Surrounded by second-rate people, and choosing for his intimate friends mainly the new rich, and now thoroughly liking the game of politics for its amusing adventure, he has retained little of his original genius except its quickness.

His intuitions are amazing. He astonished great soldiers in the war by his premonstrations. Lord Milner, a cool critic, would sit by the sofa of the dying Dr. Jameson telling how Mr. Lloyd George was right again and again when all the soldiers were wrong. Lord Rhondda, who disliked him greatly and rather despised him, told me how often Mr. Lloyd George put heart into a Cabinet that was really trembling on the edge of

despair. It seems true that he never once doubted
ultimate victory, and, what is much more remarkable,
never once failed to read the German's mind.

I think that the doom that has fallen upon him
comes in some measure from the amusement he takes in
his mental quickness, and the reliance he is sometimes
apt to place upon it. A quick mind may easily be a
disorderly mind. Moreover quickness is not one of
the great qualities. It is indeed seldom a partner with
virtue. Morality appears on the whole to get along
better without it. According to Landor, it is the
talent most open to suspicion:

Quickness is among the least of the mind's properties,
and belongs to her in almost her lowest state: nay, it doth
not abandon her when she is driven from her home, when
she is wandering and insane. The mad often retain it; the
liar has it; the cheat has it: we find it on the racecourse and
at the card-table: education does not give it, and reflection
takes away from it.

When we consider what Mr. Lloyd George might
have done with the fortunes of humanity we are able
to see how great is his distance from the heights of
moral grandeur.

He entered the war with genuine passion. He swept
thousands of hesitating minds into those dreadful fur-
naces by the force of that passion. From the first no
man in the world sounded so ringing a trumpet note of
moral indignation and moral aspiration. Examine his
earlier speeches and in all of them you will find that his

passion to destroy Prussian militarism was his passion to recreate civilization on the foundations of morality and religion. He was Peace with a sword. Germany had not so much attempted to drag mankind back to barbarism as opened a gate through which mankind might march to the promised land. Lord Morley was almost breaking his heart with despair, and to this day regards Great Britain's entrance into the war as a mistake. Sir Edward Grey was agonizing to avert war; but Mr. Lloyd George was among the first to see this war as the opportunity of a nobler civilization. Destroy German militarism, shatter the Prussian tradition, sweep away dynastic autocracies, and what a world would result for labouring humanity!

This was 1914. But soon after the great struggle had begun the note changed. Hatred of Germany and fear for our Allies' steadfastness occupied the foremost place in his mind. Victory was the objective and his definition of victory was borrowed from the prize-ring. A better world had to wait. He became more and more reckless. There was a time when his indignation against Lord Kitchener was almost uncontrollable. For Mr. Asquith he never entertained this violent feeling, but gradually lost patience with him, and only decided that he must go when procrastination appeared to jeopardize "a knock-out blow."

Anyone who questioned the cost of the war was a timid soul. What did it matter what the war cost so long as victory was won? Anyone who questioned the

utter recklessness which characterized the Ministry of
Munitions was a mere fault-finder. I spoke to him once
of the unrest in factories, where boys could earn £15 and
£16 a week by merely watching a machine they knew
nothing about, while the skilled foremen, who alone
could put those machines right, and who actually
invented new tools to make the new machines of the
inventors, were earning only the fixed wage of fifty
shillings a week. I thought this arrangement made for
unrest and must prove dangerous after the war. So
eager, so hot was his mind on the end, that he missed
the whole point of my remark. "What does it matter,"
he exclaimed impatiently, "what we pay those boys
as long as we win the war?"

And the end of it was the humiliation of the General
Election in 1918. Where was the new world, then?
He was conscious only of Lord Northcliffe's menace.
Germany must pay and the Kaiser must be tried!
There was no trumpet note in those days, and there has
been no trumpet note since. Imagine how Gladstone
would have appealed to the conscience of his countrymen! Was there ever a greater opportunity in statesmanship? After a victory so tremendous, was there
any demand on the generosity of men's souls which
would not gladly have been granted? The long struggle
between capital and labour, which tears every state in
two, might have been ended: the heroism and self-
sacrifice of the war might have been carried forward
to the labours of reconstruction: the wounds of Europe

might have been healed by the charities of God almost to the transfiguration of humanity.

Germany must pay for the war!—and he knew that by no possible means could Germany be made to pay that vast account without the gravest danger of unemployment here and Bolshevism in Central Europe! The Kaiser must be tried!—and he knew that the Kaiser never would be tried!

Millennium dipped below the horizon, and the child's riding-whip which Lord Northcliffe cracks when he is overtaken by a fit of Napoleonic indigestion assumed for the Prime Minister the proportions of the Damoclesian sword. He numbered himself among the Tououpinambos, those people who "have no name for God and believe that they will get into Paradise by practising revenge and eating up their enemies."

I can see nothing sinister in what some people regard as his plots against those who disagree with him. He tries, first of all, to win them to his way of thinking: if he fails, and if they still persist in attacking him, he proceeds to destroy them. It is all part of life's battle! But one would rather that the Prime Minister of Great Britain was less mixed up in journalism, less afraid of journalism, and less occupied, however indirectly, in effecting, or striving to effect, editorial changes. His conduct in the last months of the war and during the election of 1918 was not only unworthy of his position but marked him definitely as a small man. He won the election, but he lost the world.

It is a great thing to have won the war, but to have won it only at the cost of more wars to come, and with the domestic problems of statesmanship multiplied and intensified to a degree of the gravest danger, this is an achievement which cannot move the lasting admiration of the human race.

The truth is that Mr. Lloyd George has gradually lost in the world of political makeshift his original enthusiasm for righteousness. He is not a bad man to the exclusion of goodness; but he is not a good man to the exclusion of badness. A woman who knows him well once described him to me in these words: "He is clever, and he is stupid; truthful and untruthful; pure and impure; good and wicked; wonderful and commonplace: in a word, he is everything." I am quite sure that he is perfectly sincere when he speaks of high aims and pure ambition; but I am equally sure that it is a relief to him to speak with amusement of trickery, cleverness, and the tolerances or the cynicisms of worldliness.

Something of the inward man may be seen in the outward. Mr. Lloyd George—I hope I may be pardoned by the importance and interest of the subject for pointing it out—is curiously formed. His head is unusually large, and his broad shoulders and deep chest admirably match his quite noble head; but below the waist he appears to dwindle away, his legs seeming to bend under the weight of his body, so that he waddles rather than walks, moving with a rolling gait which is

rather like a seaman's.   He is, indeed, a giant mounted on a dwarf's legs.

So in like manner one may see in him a soul of eagle force striving to rise above the earth on sparrow's wings.

That he is attractive to men of a high order may be seen from the devotion of Mr. Philip Kerr; that he is able to find pleasure in a far lower order of men may be seen from his closer friendships.   It is impossible to imagine Mr. Gladstone enjoying the society of Mr. Lloyd George's most constant companion although that gentleman is a far better creature than the cause of his fortunes; and one doubts if Lord Beaconsfield would have trusted even the least frank of his private negotiations to some of the men who enjoy the Prime Minister's political confidence.   Nor can Mr. Lloyd George retort that he makes use of all kinds of energy to get his work done, for one knows very well that he is far more at his ease with these third-rate people than with people of a higher and more intellectual order.   For culture he has not the very least of predilections; and the passion of morality becomes more and more one of the pious memories of his immaturity.

Dr. Clifford would be gladly, even beautifully, welcomed; but after an hour an interruption by Sir William Sutherland would be a delightful relief.

M. Clemenceau exclaimed of him, lifting up amazed hands, "I have never met so ignorant a man as Lloyd

George!" A greater wit said of him, "I believe Mr. Lloyd George *can* read, but I am perfectly certain he never does."

I detect in him an increasing lethargy both of mind and body. His passion for the platform, which was once more to him than anything else, has almost gone. He enjoys well enough a fight when he is in it, but to get him into a fight is not now so easy as his hangers-on would wish. The great man is tired, and, after all, evolution is not to be hurried. He loves his arm-chair, and he loves talking. Nothing pleases him for a longer spell than desultory conversation with someone who is content to listen, or with someone who brings news of electoral chances. Of course he is a tired man, but his fatigue is not only physical. He mounted up in youth with wings like an eagle, in manhood he was able to run without weariness, but the first years of age find him unable to walk without faintness—the supreme test of character. If he had been able to keep the wings of his youth I think he might have been almost the greatest man of British history. But luxury has invaded, and cynicism; and now a cigar in the depths of an easy-chair, with Miss Megan Lloyd George on the arm, and a clever politician on the opposite side of the hearth, this is pleasanter than any poetic vapourings about the millennium.

If only he could rise from that destroying chair, if only he could fling off his vulgar friendships, if only he could trust himself to his vision, if only he could believe

once again passionately in truth, and justice, and goodness, and the soul of the British people!

One wonders if the angels in heaven will ever forgive
his silence at a time when the famished children of
Austria, many of them born with no bones, were dying like flies at the shrivelled breasts of their starving
mothers. One wonders if the historian sixty years
hence will be able to forgive him his rebuff to the first
genuine democratic movement in Germany during the
war. His responsibility to God and to man is enormous
beyond reckoning. Only the future can decide his
place here and hereafter. It is a moral universe, and,
sooner or later, the judgments of God manifest themselves to the eyes of men.

One seems to see in him an illustrious example both
of the value and perils of emotionalism. What power
in the world is greater, controlled by moral principle?
What power so dangerous, when moral earnestness
ceases to inspire the feelings?

Before the war he did much to quicken the social
conscience throughout the world; at the outbreak of war
he was the very voice of moral indignation; and during
the war he was the spirit of victory; for all this, great is
our debt to him. But he took upon his shoulders a
responsibility which was nothing less than the future of
civilization, and here he trusted not to vision and conscience but to compromise, makeshift, patches, and the
future of civilization is still dark indeed.

This I hope may be said on his behalf when he stands

at the bar of history, that the cause of his failure to serve the world as he might have done, as Gladstone surely would have done, was due rather to a vulgarity of mind for which he was not wholly responsible than to any deliberate choice of a cynical partnership with the powers of darkness.

2

LORD CARNOCK

LORD CARNOCK, 1ST BARON
(ARTHUR NICOLSON, 11TH BART.)

Born, 1849. Educ.: Rugby and Oxford; in Foreign Office, 1870–74; Secretary to Earl Granville, 1872–74; Embassy at Berlin, 1874–76; at Pekin, 1876–78; Chargé, Athens, 1884–85; Teheran, 1885–88; Consul-General, Budapest, 1888-93; Embassy, Constantinople, 1894; Minister, Morocco, 1895–1904; Ambassador, Madrid, 1904–5; Ambassador, Russia, 1905–10; Under Secretary for Foreign Affairs, 1910–16. Author of the *History of the German Constitution*, 1873.

LORD CARNOCK

CHAPTER II

LORD CARNOCK

" Usually the greatest boasters are the smallest workers. The deep rivers pay a larger tribute to the sea than shallow brooks, and yet empty themselves with less noise."—SECKER.

ONE evening in London I mentioned to a man well versed in foreign affairs that I was that night meeting Lord Carnock at dinner. "Ah!" he exclaimed, "the man who made the war."

I mentioned this remark to Lord Carnock. He smiled and made answer, "What charming nonsense!" I asked him what he thought was in my friend's mind. "Oh, I see what he meant," was the answer; "but it is a wild mind that would say any one man made the war." Later, after some remarks which I do not feel myself at liberty to repeat, he said: "Fifty years hence I think a historian will find it far more difficult than we do now to decide who made the war."

If Lord Carnock were to write his memoirs, not only would that volume help the historian to follow the immediate causes of the war to one intelligible origin, but it would also afford the people of England an opportunity of seeing the conspicuous difference between a statesman of the old school and a politician of these latter days.

When I think of this most amiable and cultivated person, and compare his way of looking at the evolution of human life with Mr. Lloyd George's way of reading the political heavens, a sentence in Bagehot's essay on Charles Dickens comes into my mind: "There is nothing less like the great lawyer, acquainted with broad principles and applying them with distinct deduction, than the attorney's clerk who catches at small point* like a dog biting at flies."

No one could be less like the popular politician of our very noisy days than this slight and gentle person whose refinement of mind reveals itself in a face almost ascetic, whose intelligence is of a wide, comprehensive, and reflecting order, and whose manner is certainly the last thing in the world that would recommend itself to the mind of an advertising agent. But there is no living politician who watched so intelligently the long beginnings of the war or knew so certainly in the days of tension that war had come, as this modest and gracious gentleman whose devotion to principle and whose quiet faith in the power of simple honour had outwitted the chaotic policy and the makeshift diplomacy of the German long before the autumn of 1914.

This may be said without revealing any State secret or breaking any private confidence:

As Sir Arthur Nicolson, our Ambassador at St. Petersburg, Lord Carnock won for England, as no other man had done before him, the love of Russia. The rulers of Russia trusted him. He was their friend in a darkness which had begun to alarm them, a darkness which made them conscious of their country's weakness, and which brought to their ears again and again the rumbles of approaching storm. Lord Carnock, sincerely loving these people, received their confidence as one friend receives the confidence of another. His advice was honourable advice. He counselled these friends to set their house in order and to stand firm in the conviction of their strength. Their finances were a chaos, their army was disorganized; let them begin in those quarters; let them bring order into their finances and let them reorganize their army.

While he was at St. Petersburg, after a wide experience in other countries, he twice saw Russia humiliated by Germany. Twice he witnessed the agony of his Russian friends in having to bow before the threats of Prussia. Remember that the rulers of Russia in those days were the most charming and cultivated people in the world, whereas the Prussian as a diplomatist was the same Prussian whom, even as an ally of ours in 1815, Croker found "very insolent, and hardly less offensive to the English than to the French."[1] The

[1] Croker writes from Paris of a visit to St. Cloud, where he found Blücher and his staff in possession: "The great hall was a common guard-house, in which the Prussians were drinking, spitting, smoking, and sleeping in all directions." Denon complained greatly of the Prussians and said he was "malheureux to have to do with a bête féroce, un animal indécrottable, le Prince Blücher."

Russians felt those humiliations as a gentleman would feel the bullying of an upstart.

Lord Carnock was at the Foreign Office in July, 1914. He alone knew that Russia would fight. For the rest of mankind, certainly for the German Kaiser, it was to be another bloodless humiliation of the Russian Bear. Admiral von Tirpitz wanted war: Bethmann-Hollweg did not. The great majority of the German people, in whom a genuine fear of Russia had increased under the astute propaganda of the War Party, hoped that the sword had only to be flashed in Russia's face for that vast barbarian to cower once again. Few statesmen in Europe thought otherwise. Sir Edward Grey, I have good reason to think, did not consider that Russia would fight. He erred with that great number of educated Germans who thought the sword had only to be rattled a little more loudly in the scabbard for Russia to weaken, and for Germany to gain, without cost, the supreme object of her policy—*an increasing ascendancy in the Balkans*. But this time Russia was ready, and this time Lord Carnock knew Russia would fight. I am not sure that Lord Carnock was not the only statesman in Europe who possessed this knowledge—the knowledge on which everything hung.

It is easy for thoughtless people, either in their hatred or love of Bolshevism, to forget that the old Russia saved France from destruction and made a greater sacrifice of her noblest life than any other nation in the great struggle. The first Russian armies, composed of the very flower of her manhood, fought with a matchless heroism, and, so fighting, delivered France from an instant defeat.

Lord Carnock may justly be said to have prepared Russia for this ordeal—for a true friend helps as well as gives good advice. But it would be a total misjudgment of his character which saw in this great work a clever stroke of diplomatic skill.

Lord Carnock was inspired by a moral principle. He saw that Russia was tempting the worst passions of Germany by her weakness. He felt this weakness to be unworthy of a country whose intellectual achievements were so great as Russia's. He had no enmity at all against the Germans. He saw their difficulties, but regretted the spirit in which they were attempting to deal with those difficulties—a spirit hateful to a nature so gentle and a mind so honourable.

He had studied for many years the Balkan problem. He knew that as Austria weakened, Germany would more and more feel the menace of Russia. He saw, over and over again, the diplomacy of the Germans thrusting Austria forward to a paramount position in the Balkans, and with his own eyes he saw the Germans in Bulgaria and Turkey fastening their hold upon those important countries. If Russia weakened, Germany would be master of the world. A strong Russia might alarm Germany and precipitate a conflict, but it was the world's chief fortress against Prussian domination.

For the sake of Russia he worked for Russia, loving her people and yet seeing the dangers of the Russian character; hoping that a self-respecting Russia might save mankind from the horrors of war and, if war came, the worse horrors of a German world-conquest. This work of his, which helped so materially to save the world, was done with clean hands. It was never the work of a war-monger. No foreigner ever exercised so great an influence in Russia, and this influence had its power in his moral nature. I had this from M. Sazonoff himself.

Such a man as Lord Carnock could not make any headway in English political life. It is worth our while to reflect that the intelligence of such men is lost to us in our home government. They have no taste for the platform, the very spirit of the political game is repellent to them, and they recoil from the self-assertion which appears to be necessary to political advancement in the House of Commons. No doubt the intelligence of men like Mr. J. H. Thomas or Mr. William Brace, certainly of Mr. Clynes, is sufficient for the crudest of our home needs, sufficient for the daily bread of our political life; but who can doubt that English politics would be lifted into a higher and altogether purer region if men like Lord Carnock were at the head of things, to provide for the spirit of man as well as for his stomach?

More and more, I think, gentlemen will stand aloof from politics—I mean, gentlemen who have received in their blood and in their training those notions of graciousness, sweetness, and nobleness which flow from centuries of piety and learning. Only here and there will such a man accept the odious conditions of our public life, inspired by a sense of duty, and prepared to endure the intolerable ugliness and dishonesty of politics for the sake of a cause which moves him with all the force of a great affection. But on the whole it is probable that the political fortunes of this great and beautiful country are committed for many years to hands which are not merely over-rough for so precious a charge, but not near clean enough for the sacredness of the English cause.

Only by indirect action, only by a much more faithful energy on the part of Aristocracy and the Church, and a far nobler realization of its responsibilities by the Press, can the ancient spirit of England make itself felt in the sordid lists of Westminster. Till then he who crows loudest will rule the roost.

LORD FISHER

BARON FISHER, ADMIRAL OF THE FLEET
(JOHN ARBUTHNOT FISHER)

Born, 1841; entered Navy, 1854; took part in 1860 in the Capture of
Canton and the Peiho Forts; Crimean War, 1855; China War, 1859-60;
Egyptian War and Bombardment of Alexandria, 1882; Lord of the
Admiralty, 1892-97; Commander-in-Chief, North American Station,
1897-99; Mediterranean Station, 1899-02; Commander-in-Chief, 1903-
1904; 1st Sea Lord, 1904-10; 1914-15; died, 1920.

BARON FISHER

CHAPTER III

LORD FISHER

"Look for a tough wedge for a tough log."
PUBLIUS SYRUS.

No man I have met ever gave me so authentic a feeling of originality as this dare-devil of genius, this pirate of public life, who more than any other Englishman saved British democracy from a Prussian domination.

It is possible to regard him as a very simple soul mastered by one tremendous purpose and by that purpose exalted to a most valid greatness. If this purpose be kept steadily in mind, one may indeed see in Lord Fisher something quite childlike. At any rate it is only when the overmastering purpose is forgotten that he can be seen with the eyes of his enemies, that is to say as a monster, a scoundrel, and an imbecile.

He was asked on one occasion if he had been a little unscrupulous in getting his way at the Admiralty. He replied that if his own brother had got in front of him when he was trying to do something for England he would have knocked that brother down and walked over his body.

Here is a man, let us be quite certain, of a most

unusual force, a man conscious in himself of powers greater than the kindest could discern in his contemporaries, a man possessed by a dæmon of inspiration. Fortunately for England this dæmon drove him in one single direction: he sought the safety, honour, and glory of Great Britain. If his contemporaries had been travelling whole-heartedly in the same direction I have no doubt that he might have figured in the annals of the Admiralty as something of a saint. But unhappily many of his associates were not so furiously driven in this direction, and finding his urgings inconvenient and vexatious they resisted him to the point of exasperation: then came the struggle, and, the strong man winning, the weaker went off to abuse him, and not only to abuse him, but to vilify him and to plot against him, and lay many snares for his feet. He will never now be numbered among the saints, but, happily for us, he was not destined to be found among the martyrs.

He has said that in the darkest hours of his struggle he had no one to support him save King Edward. Society was against him; half the Admiralty was crying for his blood; the politicians wavered from one side to the other; only the King stood fast and bade him go on with a good heart. When he emerged from this tremendous struggle his hands may not have been as clean as the angels could have wished; but the British Navy was no longer scattered over the pleasant waters of the earth, was no longer thinking chiefly of its paint and brass, was no longer a pretty sight from Mediterranean or Pacific shores—it was almost the dirtiest thing to be seen in the North Sea, and quite the deadliest thing in the whole world as regards gunnery.

This was Lord Fisher's superb service. He foresaw and he prepared. Not merely the form of the Fleet was revolutionized under his hand, but its spirit. The British Navy was baptized into a new birth with the pea-soup of the North Sea.

When this great work was accomplished he ordered a ship to be built which should put the Kiel Canal out of business for many years. That done, and while the Germans were spending the marks which otherwise would have built warships in widening and deepening this channel to the North Sea, Lord Fisher wrote it down that war with Germany would come in 1914, and that Captain Jellicoe would be England's Nelson.

From that moment he lost something of the hard and almost brutal expression which had given so formidable a character to his face. He gave rein to his natural humour. He let himself go; quoted more freely from the Bible, asserted more positively that the English people are the lost tribes of Israel, and waited for Armageddon with a humorous eye on the perturbed face of Admiral Tirpitz.

In July, 1914, he was out of office. A telegram came to him from Mr. Winston Churchill, First Lord of the Admiralty, requesting to see him urgently. Lord Fisher refused to see him, believing that Mr. Churchill had jockeyed Mr. Reginald McKenna out of the Admiralty—Mr. McKenna who had most bravely, nay heroically, stood by the naval estimates in face of strong Cabinet opposition. On this ground he refused to meet Mr. Churchill. But a telegram from Mr. McKenna followed, urging him to grant this interview, and the meeting took place, a private meeting away from London. Mr. Churchill informed Lord Fisher of the facts of the European situation, and asked him for advice. The facts were sufficient to convince Lord Fisher that the tug-o'-war between Germany and England had begun. He told Mr. Churchill that he must do three things, and do them all by telegram before he left that room: he must mobilize the Fleet, he must buy the Dreadnoughts building for Turkey, and he must appoint Admiral Jellicoe Commander-in-Chief of the Grand Fleet. To do either of the first two was a serious breach of Cabinet discipline; to do the last was to offend a string of Admirals senior to Admiral Jellicoe. Mr. Churchill hesitated. Lord Fisher insisted. "What does it matter," he said, "whom you offend?—the fate of England depends on you. Does it matter if they shoot you, or hang you, or send you to the Tower, so long as England is saved?" And Mr. Churchill did as he was bidden—the greatest act in his life, and perhaps one of the most courageous acts in the history of statesmanship. Lord Fisher said afterwards, "You may not like Winston, but he has got the heart of a lion."

Thus was England saved, and Germany doomed. Before war was declared the British Fleet held the seas, and in command of that Fleet was the quickest working brain in the Navy.

On one occasion, during the dark days of the war, I was lunching at the Admiralty with Lord Fisher, who had then been recalled to office. He appeared rather dismal, and to divert him I said, "I've got some good news for you—we are perfectly safe and Germany is beaten." He looked up from his plate and regarded me with lugubrious eyes. I then told him that Lord Kitchener had been down at Knole with the Sackvilles and had spent a whole day in taking blotting-paper impressions of the beautiful mouldings of the doors for his house at Broome. "Does that make you feel safe?" he demanded; and then, pointing to a maidservant at the sideboard, he added, "See that parlourmaid?— well, she's leaving; yesterday I spent two hours at Mrs. Hunt's registry office interviewing parlourmaids. Now, do you feel safe?"

His return to the Admiralty brought him no happiness—save when he sent Admiral Sturdee to sea to avenge the death of Admiral Cradock. He was perhaps too insistent on victory, a crushing and overwhelming victory, for a Fleet on which hung the whole safety of the Allies, and a Fleet which had experienced the deadly power of the submarine. He was certainly not too old for work. To the last, looking as if he was bowed down to the point of exhaustion by his labours, he outworked all his subordinates.   As for energy, he would have hanged I know not how many admirals if he had been in power during the last stages of the war.

His experience of Downing Street filled him up to the brim with contempt for politicians. It was not so much their want of brains that troubled him, but their total lack of character. Only here and there did he come across a man who had the properties of leadership in even a minor degree: for the most part they had no eyes for the horizon or for the hills whence cometh man's salvation; they were all ears, and those ears were leaned to the ground to catch the rumbles of political emergencies.

To find men at the head of so great a nation with no courage in the heart, with no exaltation of captaincy in the soul, without even the decency to make sacrifices for principle, made him bitterly contemptuous. At first he could scarcely bridle his rage, but as years went on he used to say that the politicians had deepened his faith in Providence. God was surely looking after England or she would have perished years agone. In his old age he ceaselessly quoted the lines of William Watson:

"Time, and the Ocean, and some fostering star
In high cabal have made us what we are";

and damned the politician with all the vigour of the Old Testament vernacular.

I have often listened to a minister's confidential gossip about Lord Fisher; nothing in these interesting confidences struck me so much as the self-satisfaction of the little minister in treating the man of destiny as an amusing lunatic.

MR. ASQUITH

THE RT. HON. HERBERT HENRY ASQUITH

Born at Morley, Yorkshire, 1852. Educ.: City of London School; Balliol College, Oxford; gained 1st class, Lit. Hum. 1874; Barrister Lincoln's Inn, 1876; Q. C. 1890; Home Sec'y, 1892–95; Ecclesiastical Commissioner, 1892–95; Chancellor of the Exchequer, 1905–8; Sec'y for War, 1914; 1st Lord of the Treasury and Prime Minister, 1908–16; LL.D. Edinburgh, Glasgow, Cambridge, Leeds, St. Andrews, and Bristol.

RT. HON. HERBERT HENRY ASQUITH

CHAPTER IV

MR. ASQUITH

"Not to mention loss of time, the tone of their feelings is lowered: they become less in earnest about those of their opinions respecting which they must remain silent in the society they frequent: they come to look upon their most elevated objects as unpractical, or at least too remote from realization to be more than a vision or a theory: and if, more fortunate than most, they retain their higher principles unimpaired, yet with respect to the persons and affairs of their own day, they insensibly adopt the modes of feeling and judgment in which they can hope for sympathy from the company they keep."
—JOHN STUART MILL.

NOTHING in Mr. Asquith's career is more striking than his fall from power: it was as if a pin had dropped.

Great men do not at any time fall in so ignominious a fashion, much less when the fate of a great empire is in the balance.

The truth is that Mr. Asquith possesses all the appearance of greatness but few of its elements. He has dignity of presence, an almost unrivalled mastery of language, a trenchant dialectic, a just and honourable mind; but he is entirely without creative power and has outgrown that energy of moral earnestness which characterized the early years of his political life.

He has never had an idea of his own. The "diffused sagacity" of his mind is derived from the wisdom of other men. He is a cistern and not a fountain.

His scholarship has made no difference to scholarship. His moral earnestness has made no difference to morality. He acquired scholarship by rote, politics by association, and morality by tradition. To none of these things did he bring the fire of original passion. The force in his youth was ambition, and the goal of his energy was success. No man ever laboured harder to judge between the thoughts of conflicting schools; few men so earnest for success ever laboured less to think for themselves. He would have made a noble judge; he might have been a powerful statesman; he could never have been a great man as Mazzini, Bismarck, and Gladstone were great men.

There are reasons for suspecting his moral qualities. When he allowed Lord Haldane to resign from the Cabinet at the shout of a few ignorant journalists he sacrificed the oldest of his friends to political exigencies. This was bad enough; but what made it worse was the appearance of heroic courage he assumed in paddling to Lord Haldane's rescue long after the tide of abuse had fallen. During the time he should have spoken to the whole nation, during the time he should have been standing sword in hand at the side of his friend, he was in negotiation with Sir Edward Carson.

It is a mistake to say that he brought England into the war. England carried Mr. Asquith into the war. The way in which politicians speak of Mr. Asquith as having "preserved the unity of the nation" in August, 1914, is index enough of the degraded condition of politics. A House of Commons that had hesitated an hour after the invasion of Belgium would have been swept out of existence by the wrath and indignation of the people. Mr. Asquith was the voice of England in that great moment of her destiny, a great and sonorous voice, but by no means her heart. He kept faction together at a moment when it was least possible for it to break apart; but he did not lead the nation into war. It was largely because he seemed to lack assurance that Lord Haldane was sacrificed. The Tories felt that Mr. Asquith would not make war whole-heartedly: they looked about for a scapegoat; Lord Haldane was chosen for this purpose by the stupidest of the Tory leaders; and the bewildered Prime Minister, with no mind of his own, and turning first to this counsellor and then to that, sacrificed the most intellectual of modern War Ministers, called Sir Edward Carson, to his side, and left the British war machine to Lord Kitchener.

We must make allowance for the time. No minister in our lifetime was confronted by such a gigantic menace. Moreover, the Cabinet was not united. Mr. Asquith came out of that tremendous ordeal creditably, but not, I think, as a great national hero. As for his conduct of the war, it was dutiful, painstaking, dignified, wise; but it lacked the impression of a creative original mind. He did not so much direct policy and inspire a nation as keep a Cabinet together. One seemed to see in him the decorative chairman of a board of

directors rather than the living spirit of the undertaking.

When the historian comes to inquire into the trivial
consequences of Mr. Asquith's fall from power he will
be forced, I think, to lift that veil which Mr. Asquith
has so jealously drawn across the privacy of his domestic
life. For although he ever lacked the essentials of
greatness, Mr. Asquith once possessed nearly all those
qualities which make for powerful leadership. Indeed
it was said in the early months of the war by the most
able of his political opponents that it passed the wit of
man to suggest any other statesman at that juncture
for the office of Prime Minister.

His judicial temperament helped him to compose
differences and to find a workable compromise. His
personal character won the respect of men who are
easily influenced by manner. There was something
about him superior to a younger generation of politicians—a dignity, a reticence, a proud and solid self-
respect. With the one exception of Mr. Alfred Spender,
a man of honour and the noblest principles, he had no
acquaintance with journalism. He never gave anybody
the impression of being an office-seeker, and there was
no one in Parliament who took less pains to secure
popularity. Above all things, he never plotted behind
closed doors; never descended to treason against a rival.

Search as men may among the records of his public
life they will fail to discover any adequate cause of his
fall from power. He was diligent in office; he took

always the highest advice in every military dispute; settled the chief difficulty at the War Office without offence to Lord Kitchener; he gave full rein to the fiery energy of Mr. Lloyd George; he was in earnest, but he was never excited; he was beset on every side, but he never failed to maintain the best traditions of English public life; he was trusted and respected by all save a clique. Even in the humiliation of the Paisley campaign he was so noble a figure that the indulgence with which he appeared to regard the rather violent aid of a witty daughter was accepted by the world as touchingly paternal—the old man did not so much lean upon the arm of his child as smile upon her high-spirited antics.

One must trespass upon the jealously guarded private life to discover the true cause of his bewildering collapse. Mr. Asquith surrendered some years ago the rigid Puritanism of early years to a domestic circle which was fatal to the sources of his original power. Anyone who compares the photographs of Mr. Asquith before and after the dawn of the twentieth century may see what I mean. In the earlier photographs his face is keen, alert, powerful, austere; you will read in it the rigidity of his Nonconformist upbringing, the serious-ness of his Puritan inheritance, all the moral earnest-ness of a nobly ambitious character. In the later photographs one is struck by an increasing expression of festivity, not by any means that beautiful radiance of the human spirit which in another man was said to make his face at the age of seventy-two "a thanksgiving for his former life and a love-letter to all mankind," but rather the expression of a mental chuckle, as though he had suddenly seen something to laugh at in the very character of the universe. The face has plumped and reddened, the light-coloured eye has acquired a twinkle, the firm mouth has relaxed into a sportive smile. You can imagine him now capping a "*mot*" or laughing deeply at a daring jest; but you cannot imagine him with profound and reverend anxiety striving like a giant to make right, reason, and the will of God prevail.

Like Mr. Lloyd George, his supplanter, he has lost the earnestness which brought him to the seats of power. A domestic circle, brilliant with the modern spirit and much occupied in sharpening the wits with epigram and audacity, has proved too much for his original stoicism. He has found recreation in the modern spirit. After the day's work there has been nothing so diverting for him as the society of young people; chatter rather than conversation has been as it were prescribed for him, and when he should have been thinking or sleeping he has been playing cards.

It is possible to argue that this complete change from the worries of the day's work has been right and proper, and that his health has been the better for it; but physical well-being can be secured by other means, and no physical well-being is worth the loss of moral power. There are some natures to whom easy-going means a descent. There are some men, and those the strongest sons of nature, for whom the kindest commandment is, "Uphill all the way."

Mr. Asquith, both by inheritance and temperament, was designed for a strenuous life, a strenuous moral life. He was never intended for anything in the nature of a *flâneur*. If he had followed his star, if he had rigorously pursued the path marked out for him by tradition and his own earliest propensities, he might have been an unpleasant person for a young ladies' tea-party and an unsympathetic person to a gathering of decadent artists; he might indeed have become as heavy as Cromwell and as inhuman as Milton; but he would never have fallen from Olympus with the lightness of thistledown.

LORD NORTHCLIFFE

LORD NORTHCLIFFE, FIRST VISCOUNT
(ALFRED CHARLES WILLIAM HARMSWORTH)

Born, 1865, in Dublin. Educ.: in Trade Schools; trained as a book-seller, and worked in the establishment of George Newnes; LL.D., Rochester Univ., U. S. A.; Proprietor of the London *Times*, *Daily Mail*, and a number of other journals; Cr. Bart. in 1904; Viscount, 1917; Chairman of the British War Mission to the United States, 1917; Director of the Aerial Transport Committee, 1917; Director of Propaganda in Enemy Countries, 1918.

LORD NORTHCLIFFE

CHAPTER V

LORD NORTHCLIFFE

" . . . We cannot say that they have a great nature, or strong, or weak, or light; it is a swift and imperious imagination which reigns with sovereign power over all their beings, which subjugates their genius, and which prescribes for them in turn those fine actions and those faults, those heights and those littlenesses, those flights of enthusiasm and those fits of disgust, which we are wrong in charging either with hypocrisy or madness."— VAUVENARGUES.

A GREAT surgeon tells me he has no doubt that Carlyle suffered all his life from a duodenal ulcer. "One may speculate," he says, "on the difference there would have been in his writings if he had undergone the operation which to-day is quite common."

This remark occurs to me when I think about Lord Northcliffe.

There is something wrong with his health. For a season he is almost boyish in high spirits, not only a charming and a most considerate host, but a spirit animated by the kindliest, broadest, and cheerfullest sympathies. Then comes a period of darkness. He seems to imagine that he may go blind, declares that he cannot eat this and that, shuts himself up from his friends, and feels the whole burden of the world pressing on his soul.

51

It is impossible to judge him as one would judge a perfectly healthy man.

The most conspicuous thing in his character is its transilience. One is aware in him of an anacoluthic quality, as if his mind suddenly stopped leaping in one direction to begin jumping in a quite contrary direction. It cannot be said that his mind *works* in any direction. It is not a trained mind. It does not know how to think and cannot support the burden of trying to think. It springs at ideas and goes off with them in haste too great for reflection. He drops these ideas when he sees an excuse for another leap. Sequence to Lord Northcliffe is a synonym for monotony. He has no *esprit de suite*. But he has leaps of real genius. An admirable title for his biography would be, "The Fits and Starts of a Discontinuous Soul." There is something of St. Vitus in his psychology. You might call him the Spring-Heeled Jack of Journalism.

A story told of one of his journalists illustrates the difficulty of dealing with so uncertain a person. Lord Northcliffe invited this journalist, let us call him Mr. H., to luncheon. They approached the lift of Carmelite House, and Lord Northcliffe drew back to let his guest enter before him—he has excellent manners and, when he is a host, is scrupulously polite to the least of people in his employment. Mr. H. approached the lift, and raising his hat and making a profound bow to the boy in charge of it, passed in before Lord Northcliffe. Nothing was said during the descent. On leaving the lift Mr. H. again raised his hat and bowed low to the boy. When they were out of earshot Lord Northcliffe remonstrated with him on his behaviour. "You shouldn't joke," he said, "with these boys, it makes discipline difficult." "Joke!" exclaimed Mr. H., "good heavens, I wasn't joking; how do I know that to-morrow he will not be the editor of the *Daily Mail?*"

This story has a real importance. It emphasizes a remarkable characteristic of Lord Northcliffe's variability. It emphasizes the romantic quality of his mind. Nothing would please him more than to discover in one of his office boys an editor for *The Times*. His own life has given him almost a novelette's passion for romance. He lives in that atmosphere. Few men I have known are so free from snobbishness or so indifferent to the petty conventions of society. The dull life of the world is hateful to him. He would make not only the journalism of the suburbs sensational, he would make the history of mankind a fairy-story.

It is difficult to understand his power in the world. He is not the great organizer that people suppose; all the organization of his business has been done by Lord Rothermere, a very able man of business; nor is he the inspirational genius one is so often asked to believe. Mr. Kennedy Jones is largely responsible for the journalistic fortunes of Lord Northcliffe.

I am disposed to think that it is the romantic quality of his mind which is the source of his power. All the men about him are unimaginative realists. He is the artist in command of the commercial mind, the poet flogging dull words into a kind of wild music. Mr. Kennedy Jones could have started any of his papers, but he could never have imparted to them that living spirit of the unexpected which has kept them so effectually from dulness. Carmelite House could give the news of the world without Lord Northcliffe's help, but without his passion for the twists and turns of the fairy-story it could never have presented that news so that it catches the attention of all classes.

I have never been conscious of greatness in Lord Northcliffe, but I have never failed to feel in his mind something unusual and remarkable. He is not an impressive person, but he is certainly an interesting person. One feels that he has preserved by some magic of temperament, not to be analyzed by the most skilful of psychologists, the spirit of boyhood. You may notice this spirit quite visibly in his face. The years leave few marks on his handsome countenance. He loves to frown and depress his lips before the camera, for, like a child, he loves to play at being somebody else, and somebody else with him is Napoleon—I am sure that he chose the title of Northcliffe so that he might sign his notes with the initial N—but when he is walking in a garden, dressed in white flannels, and looking as if he had just come from a Turkish bath, he has all the appearance of a youth. It is a tragedy that a smile so agreeable should give way at times to a frown as black as midnight; that the freshness of his complexion should yield to an almost jaundiced yellow; and that the fun and frolic of the spirit should flee away so suddenly and for such long periods before the witch of melancholy.

Of his part in the history of the world no historian will be able to speak with unqualified approval. His political purpose from beginning to end, I am entirely convinced, has been to serve what he conceives to be the highest interests of his country. I regard him in the matter of intention as one of the most honourable and courageous men of the day. But he is reckless in the means he employs to achieve his ends. I should say he has no moral scruples in a fight, none at all; I doubt very much if he ever asks himself if anything is right or wrong. I should say that he has only one question to ask of fate before he strips for a fight—is this thing going to be Success or Failure?

In many matters of great importance he has been right, so right that we are apt to forget the number of times he has been wrong. Whether he may not be charged in some measure at least with the guilt of the war, whether he is not responsible for the great bitterness of international feelings which characterized Europe during the last twenty years, is a question that must be left to the historian. But it is already apparent that for want of balance and a moral continuity in his direction of policy Lord Northcliffe has done nothing to elevate the public mind and much to degrade it. He has jumped from sensation to sensation.

The opportunity for a fight has pleased him more than the object of the fight has inspired him. He has never seen in the great body of English public opinion a spirit to be patiently and orderly educated towards noble ideals, but rather a herd to be stampeded of a sudden in the direction which he himself has as suddenly conceived to be the direction of success.

The true measure of his shortcomings may be best taken by seeing how a man exercising such enormous power, power repeated day by day, and almost at every hour of the day, might have prepared the way for disarmament and peace, might have modified the character of modern civilization, might have made ostentation look like a crime, might have brought capital and labour into a sensible partnership, and might have given to the moral ideals of the noblest sons of men if not an intellectual impulse at least a convincing advertisement.

The moral and intellectual condition of the world, a position from which only a great spiritual palingenesis can deliver civilization, is a charge on the sheet which Lord Northcliffe will have to answer at the seat of judgment. He has received the price of that condition in·the multitudinous pence of the people; consciously or unconsciously he has traded on their ignorance, ministered to their vulgarities, and inflamed the lowest and most corrupting of their passions: if they had had another guide his purse would be empty.

All the same, it is the greatest mistake for his enemies

to declare that he is nothing better than a cynical egoist trading on the enormous ignorance of the English middle-classes. He is a boy, full of adventure, full of romance, and full of whims, seeing life as the finest fairy-tale in the world, and enjoying every incident that comes his way, whether it be the bitterest and most cruel of fights or the opportunity for doing some-one a romantic kindness.

You may see the boyishness of his nature in the devotion with which he threw himself first into bicycling, then into motoring, and then into flying. He loves machinery. He loves every game which involves physical risk and makes severe demands on courage. His love of England is not his love of her merchants and workmen, but his love of her masculine youth.

He has been generosity itself to his brothers, with all of whom he does not, unfortunately, get on as well as one could wish. The most beautiful thing in his life is the love he cherishes for his mother, and nothing delights him so much as taking away her breath by acts of astonishing devotion. A man so generous and so boyish may make grave mistakes, but he cannot be a deliberately bad man.

MR. ARTHUR BALFOUR

THE RT. HON. ARTHUR JAMES BALFOUR

Born in Scotland 1848; s. of Jas. M. Balfour and Lady Blanche Cecil; nephew of the late Marquis of Salisbury and therefore 1st cousin to the present Marquis, Lord Robert Cecil, and Lord Hugh Cecil. Educ.: Eton and Trinity Coll., Cambridge; LL.D. Edinburgh, St. Andrews, Cambridge, Dublin, Glasgow, Manchester, Liverpool, Birmingham, Bristol, Sheffield, Columbia (New York); D.C.L. Oxford. M.P. for Hertford, 1874–85; Private Sec'y to his uncle, the late Marquis of Salisbury, 1878–80; served on Mission to Berlin with Salisbury and Beaconsfield, 1878; Privy Councillor, 1885; President of Local Government Board, 1885–86; Sec'y for Scotland, 1886–87; Lord Rector, St. Andrews, 1886; Sec'y for Ireland, 1887–91; Lord Rector, Glasgow, 1890; Chancellor of Edinburgh since 1891; First Lord of Treasury, 1891–92; President British Association, 1904; Prime Minister, 1902–1905; Leader of the Commons, 1895–1906; 1st Lord of the Admiralty 1915–16; Head of British Mission to America, 1917; Author of a series of philosophical and economic works.

RT. HON. ARTHUR JAMES BALFOUR

CHAPTER VI

MR. ARTHUR BALFOUR

"A sceptre once put into the hand, the grip is instinctive; and he who is firmly seated in authority soon learns to think security and not progress, the highest lesson of statecraft."—J. R. LOWELL.

IN one of the *Tales* Crabbe introduces to us a young lady, Arabella by name, who read Berkeley, Bacon, Hobbes, and Locke and was such a prodigy of learning that she became the wonder of the fair town in which, as he tells us, she shone like a polished brilliant. From that town she reaped, and to that town she gave, renown:

> And strangers coming, all were taught t'admire
> The learned Lady, and the lofty Spire.

One feels that in Mr. Balfour there is something of both the learned Lady and the lofty Spire. He is at once spinsterish and architectural. I mean that he is a very beautiful object to look at, and at the same time a frustrated and perverse nature. Moreover his learning partakes of a drawing-room character, while his loftiness dwindles away to a point which affords no foothold for the sons of man. One may look up to him now and again, but a constant regard would be rewarded by nothing more serviceable to the admirer than a stiff neck. He points upward indeed, but to follow his direction is to discover only the void of etheric vacancy. Like his learning, which may astonish the simple, but which hardly illuminates the student, his virtues leave one cold. Someone who knows him well said to me once, "He is no Sir Galahad. Week-ending and London society have deteriorated his fibre."

He began life well, but he has slackness in his blood and no vital enthusiasm in his heart. His career has been a descent. He has taken things—ethically and industrially—easily, too easily.

It is a pity that Nature forgot to bestow upon him those domestic motions of the heart which humanize the mind and beautify character, for in many ways he was fitted to play a great part in affairs of State and with real emotion in his nature would have made an ideal leader of the nation during the struggle with Germany. He is a conspicuous example of the value of sensibility, for lacking this one quality he has entirely failed to reach the greatness to which his many gifts entitled him.

Few men can be so charming: no man can be more impressive. His handsome appearance, his genial manner, his distinguished voice, his eagerness and playfulness in conversation, all contribute to an impression of personality hardly equalled at the present time. He might easily pass for the perfect ideal of the gentleman. In a certain set of society he remains to this day a

veritable prince of men.   And his tastes are pure, and
his life is wholesome.

A lady of my acquaintance was once praising to its
mother a robust and handsome infant who could boast
a near relationship with Mr. Arthur Balfour.   "Yes,"
said the mother, with criticism in her eyes and voice,
"I think he is a nice child, but we rather fear he lacks
the Balfourian manner."   Even in childhood!

This Balfourian manner, as I understand it, has its
roots in an attitude of mind—an attitude of convinced
superiority which insists in the first place on complete
detachment from the enthusiasms of the human race,
and in the second place on keeping the vulgar world
at arm's length.

It is an attitude of mind which a critic or a cynic
might be justified in assuming, for it is the attitude of
one who desires rather to observe the world than to
shoulder any of its burdens; but it is a posture of
exceeding danger to anyone who lacks tenderness or
sympathy, whatever his purpose or office may be, for it
tends to breed the most dangerous of all intellectual
vices, that spirit of self-satisfaction which Dostoievsky
declares to be the infallible mark of an inferior mind.

To Mr. Arthur Balfour this studied attitude of aloof-
ness has been fatal, both to his character and to his
career.   He has said nothing, written nothing, done
nothing, which lives in the heart of his countrymen.
To look back upon his record is to see a desert, and a
desert with no altar and with no monument, without

even one tomb at which a friend might weep. One does not say of him, "He nearly succeeded there," or "What a tragedy that he turned from this to take up that"; one does not feel for him at any point in his career as one feels for Mr. George Wyndham or even for Lord Randolph Churchill; from its outset until now that career stretches before our eyes in a flat and uneventful plain of successful but inglorious and ineffective self-seeking.

There is one signal characteristic of the Balfourian manner which is worthy of remark. It is an assumption in general company of a most urbane, nay, even a most cordial spirit. I have heard many people declare at a public reception that he is the most gracious of men, and seen many more retire from shaking his hand with a flush of pride on their faces as though Royalty had stooped to inquire after the measles of their youngest child. Such is ever the effect upon vulgar minds of geniality in superiors: they love to be stooped to from the heights.

But this heartiness of manner is of the moment only, and for everybody; it manifests itself more personally in the circle of his intimates and is irresistible in week-end parties; but it disappears when Mr. Balfour retires into the shell of his private life and there deals with individuals, particularly with dependents. It has no more to do with his spirit than his tail-coat and his white tie. Its remarkable impression comes from its unexpectedness; its effect is the shock of surprise. In public he is ready to shake the whole world by the hand, almost to pat it on the shoulder; but in private he is careful to see that the world does not enter even the remotest of his lodge gates.

"The truth about Arthur Balfour," said George Wyndham, "is this: he knows there's been one ice-age, and he thinks there's going to be another."

Little as the general public may suspect it, the charming, gracious, and cultured Mr. Balfour is the most egotistical of men, and a man who would make almost any sacrifice to remain in office. It costs him nothing to serve under Mr. Lloyd George; it would have cost him almost his life to be out of office during a period so exciting as that of the Great War. He loves office more than anything this world can offer; neither in philosophy nor music, literature nor science, has he ever been able to find rest for his soul. It is profoundly instructive that a man with a real talent for the noblest of those pursuits which make solitude desirable and retirement an opportunity should be so restless and dissatisfied, even in old age, outside the doors of public life.

The most serious effect upon his character of this central selfishness may be seen in his treatment of George Wyndham. Mr. Balfour has had only one friend in his parliamentary life, Alfred Lyttelton, but George Wyndham came nearer to his affections than any other man in the Unionist Party, and was at one time Mr. Balfour's devoted admirer. Nevertheless,

5

in the hour of his tragedy, in the hour which broke his heart and destroyed his career, Mr. Balfour, who should have championed him against the wolves of the Party, and might, I verily believe, have saved both him and Ireland, turned away his face and rendered homage to political opportunism. Wyndham's grave and the present condition of Ireland stand as sorrowful reminders of that unworthy act.

Wyndham was by no means a first-rate politician, but he was a sincere man, something too of a genius, and I think there was genuine inspiration in his method of solving the Irish question.

This incident reveals in Mr. Balfour a capacity for meanness which rather darkens his good qualities. It prevents one from believing that his conduct has always been guided by noble and disinterested motives. The historian might have said that although he mistook astuteness and adroitness in parliamentary debate for statesmanship, and although he accomplished nothing for the good of his country, he yet lent a certain dignity and nobleness to public life at a time when it was besieged by new forces in democracy having no reverence for tradition and little respect for good manners; but when the full truth of the Wyndham incident is related it will be difficult for the historian to avoid a somewhat harsh judgment on Mr. Balfour's character.

Nor does the Wyndham incident stand alone. His treatment of Mr. Ritchie and Lord George Hamilton was very bad. Then there was the case of Joseph

Chamberlain, who had good reason never to forgive him. Some day Mr. Asquith (or will it be Mrs. Asquith) may tell the story of dealings with Mr. Balfour which were not of a handsome character. The more these things are revealed the worse I think it will be for Mr. Balfour's character.

But such is the personal effect of the man that even those whom he has treated badly never bring any public charge against him. With the exception of Mr. Asquith, and Joseph Chamberlain, all forgave him, and even sought to fin d excuses for his inexplicable lapse. But I am inclined to think that this indicates weakness on the part of the victim rather than grace on the part of the victimizer.

There are other ways in which his lack of sensibility manifests itself in an unpleasant fashion. He is so self-absorbed that he appears to be wholly unaware of those who minister to his comfort. Of his servants he never knows the least detail, not even their names, and even a devoted secretary who has served him faithfully for many years may find himself treated almost as a stranger in a moment of need. I fear it must be said that in financial matters Mr. Balfour is as close-fisted as any miser, although I believe that this meanness has its rise, not so much in avariciousness as in a total incapacity to realize the importance of money to other people.

It has been said that the whole history of philosophical thought is an attempt to separate the object and the subject. Mr. Balfour appears to have made this separation complete. For him there is no object. His mind has embraced his subjective self, and has not merely refused the fruitless effort of attempting to stand outside its functions in order to perceive its own perceptions, but, abandoning the unperceived perceptions and the inactive activities of ultimate reality, it has canonized its own functions and deified its own subjective universe. So complete, indeed, is this separation that he can scarcely be called selfish, since for him there exists no objective field for the operation of unselfishness.

I lament this self-absorption of Mr. Balfour as much as I lament in his cousin Lord Robert Cecil the lack of the fighting qualities of leadership. To no man of the Unionist Party after the death of Lord Beaconsfield and Lord Salisbury have more hopeful opportunities presented themselves for creative statesmanship. He might have settled the Irish Question. He might have avoided the Boer War, in the conduct of which he behaved with real nobleness at the beginning. He might have saved Germany from her own warmongers. In any case he might have led the Unionist Party towards construction and so have prevented the slap-dash methods at reform set going by Mr. Lloyd George after a long and irritating period of Tory pottering. For few men in modern times have exercised so great a fascination over that curious and easily satisfied body, the House of Commons, and no man in the public life of our times has enjoyed a more powerful prestige in the constituencies. Indeed, he stood for many years as the most dignified and honourable figure in the public life of Great Britain, and his influence in politics during the first part of that period was without serious rivalry.

It must not be forgotten, too, that in the days of "bloody Balfour" he was not merely chivalrous, but even Quixotic, in taking upon himself the mistakes and misdoings of his subordinates in Ireland. He certainly had the makings of a chivalrous figure, and perhaps even a great man. One thinks that he began his descent unconsciously, and that carelessness rather than any inherent badness led gradually to an egoism which has proved fatal to his powers and to his character.

To the self-aborbed, vision is impossible. Mr. Balfour, unable to penetrate the future, has lived from day to day, enjoying the game of politics for the fun of confounding critics and managing colleagues, enjoying too the privilege and dignity of power, but never once feeling the call of the future, or experiencing one genuine desire to leave the world better than he found it. And now he ends his political career clinging to a decorative office under the leadership of Mr. Lloyd George.

At the end of his Gifford Lectures, after an argument which induced one of his listeners to say that he had *a stammer in his thoughts*, Mr. Balfour announced his faith in God. One may recall Pascal's exclamation, "How far it is from believing in God to loving Him!"

I have always thought it significant of his true nature that Mr. Balfour should be one of the worst offenders in that unlovely Front Bench habit of putting his feet up on the Clerk's table. The last time I was in the House of Commons Mr. J. H. Thomas was lying back on the Opposition Front Bench with his legs in the air and his muddy boots crossed on the table. The boorishness of this attitude struck my companion very sharply. But I pointed out to him that the difference between Mr. Thomas, the Labour member, and Mr. Balfour, the great gentleman, was merely a size in boots.

LORD KITCHENER

LORD KITCHENER OF KHARTOUM

Born, 1846; entered Army, 1866; Colonel, 1899; Burmah Campaign, 1891; Viscount, 1914; Baron, 1914; Earl, 1914; Sec'y for War, 1914; died, 1917.

LORD KITCHENER

CHAPTER VII

LORD KITCHENER

"I never knew a man so fixed upon doing what he considered his duty."—
CROKER PAPERS.

SOON after he had taken his chair at the War Office,
Lord Kitchener received a call from Mr. Lloyd George.
The politician had come to urge the appointment of
denominational chaplains for all the various sects
represented in the British Army.

Lord Kitchener was opposed to the idea, which
seemed to him irregular, unnecessary, and expensive,
involving a waste of transport, rations, and clerks'
labour. But Mr. Lloyd George stuck to his sectarian
guns, and was so insistent, especially in respect of
Presbyterians, that at last the Secretary of State for
War yielded in this one case. He took up his pen
rather grudgingly and growled out, "Very well: you
shall have a Presbyterian." Then one of his awkward
smiles broke up the firmness of his bucolic face.
"Let's see," he asked; "Presbyterian?—how do you
spell it?"

This was one of his earliest adventures with politicians, and he ended it with a sly cut at unorthodoxy.

A little later came another political experience which afforded him real insight into this new world of Party faction, one of those experiences not to be lightly dismissed with a jest.

He discovered at the War Office that preparations had been made for just such an emergency as had now occurred. The thoughtfulness and thoroughness of this work struck him with surprise, and he inquired the name of its author. He was told that Lord Haldane had made these preparations. "Haldane!" he exclaimed; "but isn't he the man who is being attacked by the newspapers?"

A chivalrous feeling which does not seem to have visited the bosoms of any of Lord Haldane's colleagues visited the bosom of this honest soldier. Someone about him who had enjoyed personal relations with various editors was dispatched to one of the most offending editors conducting the campaign against Lord Haldane with the object of stopping this infamous vendetta.

"I know what you say is true," replied this editor, "and I regret the attack as much as Lord Kitchener does; but I have received my orders and they come from so important a quarter that I dare not disobey them." He gave Lord Kitchener's emissary the name of a much respected leader of the Unionist Party.

Thus early in his career at the War Office Lord Kitchener learnt that the spirit of the public school does not operate in Westminster and that politics are a dirty business.

At no time in his life was Lord Kitchener "a race-horse amongst cows," as the Greeks put it, being, even in his greatest period, of a slow, heavy, and laborious turn of mind; but when he entered Mr. Asquith's Cabinet he was at least an honest man amongst lawyers. He was a great man; wherever he sat, to borrow a useful phrase, was the head of the table; but this greatness of his, not being the full greatness of a complete man, and having neither the support of a keen intellect nor the foundations of a strong moral character, wilted in the atmosphere of politics, and in the end left him with little but the frayed cloak of his former reputation.

There is no doubt that his administration of the War Office was not a success. In all important matters of strategy he shifted his ground from obstinacy to sulkiness, yielding where he should not have yielded at all, and yielding grudgingly where to yield without the whole heart was fatal to success: in the end he was among the drifters, "something between a hindrance and a help," and the efforts to get rid of him were perhaps justified, although Mr. Asquith's policy of curtailing his autocracy on the occasions when he was abroad had the greater wisdom.

I shall not trouble to correct the popular idea of Lord Kitchener's character beyond saying that he was the last man in the world to be called a machine, and that he solemnly distrusted the mechanism of all organizations. He was first and last an out-and-out individualist, a

believer in men, a hater of all systems. As Sir Ian
Hamilton has said, wherever he saw organization his
first instinct was to smash it. I think his autocracy
at the War Office might have been of greater service
to the country if all the trained thinkers of the Army,
that small body of brilliant men, had not been in
France. Even in his prime Lord Kitchener was the
most helpless of men without lieutenants he could
trust to do his bidding or to improve upon it in the
doing.

It will better serve the main purpose of this book to
suggest in what particulars the real greatness of this
once glorious and finally pathetic figure came to suffer
shipwreck at the hands of the politicians.

Lord Kitchener's greatness was the indefinable
greatness of personality. He was not a clever man.
He had no gifts of any kind. In the society of scholars
he was mum and among the lovers of the beautiful he
cut an awkward figure. At certain moments he had
curious flashes of inspiration, but they came at long
intervals and were seldom to be had in the day of
drudgery, when his mind was not excited. On the
whole his intelligence was of a dull order, plodding
heavily through experience, mapping the surface of life
rather than penetrating any of its mysteries, making
slowly quite sure of one or two things rather than
grasping the whole problem at a stroke.

But there was one movement in his character which
developed greatness and by its power brought him to

wonderful success and great honour; this was a deep, an unquestioning, a religious sense of duty.

He started life with a stubborn ambition. As he went along he felt the rightness of duty, and married his ambition to this Spartan virtue. He remained in most respects as selfish a man as ever lived, as selfish as a greedy schoolboy; nevertheless by the power of his single virtue, to which he was faithful up to his last moments on this earth, he was able to sacrifice his absorbing self-interest to the national welfare even in a political atmosphere which sickened him at every turn.

You may see what I mean by considering that while he longed for nothing so much in later life as the possession of Broome Park, and that while his selfishness stopped hardly at anything to enrich that house with pictures, china, and furniture, and that while he would shamelessly hint for things in the houses of the people who were entertaining him, even in the houses of his own subordinates, until the weaker or the more timorous gave him the object of his covetousness, nevertheless for the sake of his country he clung to the uncongenial chair in Whitehall, not merely working like a cart-horse for what he considered to be his nation's good, but suffering without public complaint of any kind, and scarcely a private grumble, all the numerous humiliations that came his way either from his own colleagues in the Cabinet or from a powerful section of the newspapers outside.

I remember hearing from the late Mr. John Bonner,

a most admirable artist in many fields, an amusing
account of an interview with Lord Kitchener which
illustrates the Field-Marshal's passion for his Kentish
home, and also sheds a telling light on the æsthetic side
of his character.

Mr. Bonner had been recommended to Lord
Kitchener, who wanted amorini scattered about the
leafy gardens at Broome. Drawings were made and
approved: a few months afterwards the amorini were
set up in the gardens.

Soon came a summons to the presence of the great
man. Mr. Bonner found him a terrible object in a
terrible rage. In his late years, be it remembered,
Lord Kitchener was not good to look upon. He
appeared a coarse, a top-heavy person; and in anger, his
cross-eyes could be painfully disconcerting.

Lord Kitchener forgot that Mr. Bonner was not
only an artist of a singularly beautiful spirit, but a
gentleman. He blazed at him. What did he mean
by sticking up those ridiculous little figures in Broome?
—what did he mean by it?—with an unpleasant reference to the account.

The poor artist, terribly affrighted, said that he
thought Lord Kitchener had seen his drawings and
approved of them. "Yes, the drawings!—but you
can't see the figures when they're up! What's the good
of something you can't see?"

The great man, it appeared at last, wanted amorini
the size of giants; a rather Rosherville taste.

"He had knowledge," said Lady Sackville, from whose beautiful house he borrowed many ideas for Broome, and would have liked to have carried off many of its possessions, particularly a William the Fourth drum which he found in his bedroom as a waste-paper receptacle; "he had knowledge but no taste."

Her daughter said to me on one occasion, "Every chair he sits in becomes a throne," referring to the atmosphere of power and dignity which surrounded him.

It is instructive, I think, to remark how a single virtue passionately held—held, I mean, with a religious sense of its seriousness—can carry even a second-class mind to genuine greatness, a greatness that can be felt if not defined. In every sense of the word greatness, as we apply it to a saint, a poet, or a statesman, Lord Kitchener was a second-class and even a third-class person; but so driving was his sense of duty that it carried him to the very forefront of national life, and but for the political atmosphere in which he had to work for the last few years of his distinguished service to the State he might have easily become one of the great and shining heroes of British history. He had no taste; but the impression he made on those who had was the impression of a great character.

How was it that his greatness, that is to say his greatness of personality, made so pitiable an end? What was lacking that this indubitable greatness should have been so easily brayed in the mortar of politics?

The answer I think is this: a single virtue can bestow greatness, and the greatness may never fail when it has time and space in which to express itself; but many virtues of intellect and character are necessary when time is of the essence of the contract, and more especially in a situation of shared responsibility.

Lord Kitchener knew many of his own failings. He was by no means a vain man. Indeed he suffered considerable pain from the knowledge that he was not the tremendous person of the popular imagination. This knowledge robbed him of self-assurance. He tried to live up to the legendary Kitchener, and so long as he could find men as brave as himself, but of swifter and more adaptable intelligence, to do his bidding, he succeeded: many of the public, indeed, believed in the legendary Kitchener up to the day of his tragic death—death, that unmistakable reality, meeting him on a journey, the object of which was to impress Russia with the legendary Kitchener. But more and more, particularly in consultation with the quick wits of politicians, he found it impossible to impersonate his reputation.

I have been told by more than one Cabinet Minister that it was impressive to see how the lightning intellects of Mr. Lloyd George and Mr. Winston Churchill again and again reduced the gigantic soldier to a stupefied and sulking silence.

A proposal would be made by a minister, and Mr. Asquith would turn to Lord Kitchener for his opinion. Lord Kitchener would say, "It's impossible," and close his lips firmly.   At this Mr. Lloyd George would attack him, pointing out the reasonableness of this proposal in swift and persuasive phrases.   Lord Kitchener, shifting on his chair, would repeat, "It's impossible."   Then in question after question Mr. Churchill would ask why it was impossible.   "It's impossible," Lord Kitchener would mumble at the end of these questions.   Finally, when nearly everybody had attempted to extract from him the reason for his refusal to countenance this proposal, he would make an impatient side movement of his head, unfold his arms, bend over the papers on the table before him, and grunt out, sometimes with a boyish smile of relief, "Oh, all right, have it your own way."

He lacked almost every grace of the spirit.   There was nothing amiable in his character.   Very few men liked him a great deal, and none I should say loved him.   I do not think he was brutal by nature, although his nature was not refined; but he cultivated a brutal manner.   He had the happiness of three or four friendships with cultivated and good women, but the beautiful creature whom he loved hungrily and doggedly, and to whom he proposed several times, could never bring herself to marry him.   I think there was no holy cf holies in his character, no sanctuaries for the finer intimacies of human life.   As Sainte-Beuve said of Rousseau, "he has at times a little goître in his voice."   One sees the fulness of his limitations by comparing him with such great figures of Indian history as the Lawrences and

6

Nicholson: in that comparison he shrinks at once to the dimensions of a colour-sergeant.

But in attempting to study a man of this nature, for our own learning, we should rather observe how notable a victory he achieved in making so much of so little than vociferate that he was not this thing or that.

He began life with no gifts from the gods; it was not in his horoscope to be either a saint or a hero; no one was less likely to create enthusiasm or to become a legend; and yet by resolutely following the road of duty, by earnestly and stubbornly striving to serve his country's interests, and by never for one moment considering in that service the safety of his own life or the making of his own fortune, this rough and ordinary man bred in himself a greatness which, magnified by the legend itself created, helped his country in one of the darkest hours, perhaps the very darkest, of its long history.

One could wish that behind this formidable greatness of personality there had been greatness of mind, greatness of character, greatness of heart, so that he might have been capable of directing the whole war and holding the politicians in leash to the conclusion of a righteous peace. But these things he lacked, and the end was what it was.

"Character," says Epicharmus, "is destiny to man." Lord Kitchener, let us assert, was faithful to his destiny. And he was something more than faithful, for he sanctified this loyalty to his own character by a devotion to his country which was pure and incorruptible. Certainly he can never be styled "the son of Cronos and Double-dealing."

LORD ROBERT CECIL

LORD ROBERT CECIL
(EDGAR ALGERNON CECIL)

Born, 1864. Educ.: at Eton and Oxford. Private Secretary to his father, the late Marquis of Salisbury, 1886–88; called to the Bar, 1887; M.P. for East Marylebone, 1906–10; for Hitchin Division of Herts, 1912; Under Secretary for Foreign Affairs, 1915–16; Assistant Secretary for Foreign Affairs, 1918; Manager of Blockade, 1916–18. Author of *Principles of Commercial Law* and *Our National Church.*

LORD ROBERT CECIL

CHAPTER VIII

LORD ROBERT CECIL

"Nothing great was ever achieved without enthusiasm."—EMERSON.

IF a novelist take for his hero an educated gentleman who expresses contempt for the licence and indecencies of modern life, it is ten to one that the critics, who confess themselves on other occasions as sick of prurient tales, will pronounce this hero to be a prig. In like manner, let a politician evince concern for the moral character of the nation and it is ten to one his colleagues in the House of Commons and his critics in the Press, and everywhere the very men most in despair of politics, will declare him to be a fanatic.

This has been the unfortunate fate of Lord Robert Cecil. He is regarded by his countrymen as unpractical. Men speak well of him, and confess willingly that he is vastly superior in character and intellect to the ruck of politicians, but nevertheless wind up their panegyrics with the regretful judgment that, alas, he is a fanatic.

It is a thousand pities, I think, that he is not a fanatic. It is for the very reason he is not fanatical that his progress in politics has been in the suburbs of the second rank. He has every quality for the first rank, and for the foremost place in that rank, save the one urging passion of enthusiasm. It is a sense of humour, an engaging sense of diffidence, a continual deviation towards a mild and gentle cynicism, it is this spirit—the very antithesis of a fanatical temper—which keeps him from leadership.

The nation has reason on its side for suspecting Lord Robert Cecil. In the mind of the British people nothing is more settled than the conviction that the conquering qualities of a great captain are courage and confidence. He has given no sign of these qualities. Nature, it would seem, has fashioned him neither pachydermatous nor pugilistic. He appears upon the platform as a gentleman makes his entrance into a drawing-room, not as a toreador leaps into the bull ring. He expresses his opinions as a gentleman expresses his views at a dinner-table, not as an ale-house politician airs his dogmatisms in the tap-room. The very qualities which give such a grace and power to his personality, being spiritual qualities, prevent him from capturing the loud and grateful loyalty of a political party.

Now, while a man like Mr. Lloyd George can only affirm his own essence by the exercise of what we may call brute force, and by making use of vulgar methods from which a person of Lord Robert Cecil's quality would naturally shrink, it is nevertheless not at all necessary for a man of noble character and greater

power to employ the same means in order to earn the
confidence of his countrymen.

What is necessary in this case is not brute force but
fanaticism, and by fanaticism I mean that spirit which
in Cromwell induced Hume to call him "this fanatical
hypocrite," and which Burke adequately defined in
saying that when men are fanatically fond of an object
they will prefer it to their own peace.

Lord Robert Cecil need not adopt the tricks of a
mountebank to achieve leadership of the British nation,
but he must contract so entire a faith in the sacred
character of his mission that all the inhibiting diffiden-
cies of his modest nature will henceforth seem to him
like the whisperings of temptation. He must cease to
watch the shifts of public opinion. He must cease
merely to recommend the probable advantage of rather
more idealism in the politics of Europe. He must act.
He must learn to know that a man cannot give a great
idea to the world without giving himself along with it.
The cause must consume the person. Individual peace
must be sacrificed for world's peace.

From the very beginning of the War Lord Robert
Cecil perceived that the need of the nation was not for
a great political leader, but for a great moral leader.
He told me so with an unforgettable emphasis, well
aware that under the public show of our national life
the heart of the British people was famishing for
such guidance. He numbered himself among those
anxiously scanning the horizon for such a leader. He

should have been instead answering the inarticulate cry of the people for that leader.

No good man of my acquaintance is more powerfully convinced of the goodness of British nature. He watches the British people with an abiding affection. He believes that they possess, even those of them who appear most degraded and sordid, the foundational virtues of Christian character—a love of justice, an instinct for kindness, and faith in truth. He knows that they are more capable than any other people in Europe of generous self-sacrifice, and that any absence of grace in their manner which must distress the superficial observer comes rather of a passion for honesty than a lack of beauty. And this knowledge of his goes with the conviction that no man will ever appeal to the British nation in vain who bases his appeal on justice, fair play, and charity. What a nation to lead! What an inspiration for a true leader!

He is convinced that no moral appeal has ever been made to the British people in vain. And yet he has never made that appeal. With grief and sorrow he watches the stampeding of the nation he so deeply admires into murderous and indiscriminate hatred of our enemies in the late war. He saw the majority of the British people's war-like mood degraded and vulgarized by the propaganda of hate. But he made no move to save the national honour. The better part, and as I firmly believe the greater part, of the nation was waiting for moral leadership: particularly were the young men

of the nation who marched to death with the purest
flame of patriotism in their hearts hungering for such
leadership; but Lord Robert Cecil, the one man in
Parliament who might have sounded that note, was
silent. The voice that should have made Britain's
glory articulate, the voice that might have brought
America into the War in 1914 and rendered Germany
from the outset a house divided against itself, was never
heard. Lord Robert Cecil looked on, and Mr. Lloyd
George sprang into the prize-ring with his battle-cry of
the knock-out blow.

I wonder if even the sublimest humility can excuse
so fatal a silence. Great powers have surely great
responsibilities.

I remember speaking to Lord Robert on one occasion
of the shooting of Miss Cavell—a brutal act which
distressed him very deeply. I said I thought we
weakened our case against Germany by speaking of that
atrocious act as a "murder," since by the rules of war,
as she herself confessed, Miss Cavell incurred the
penalty of death. He replied: "What strikes me as
most serious in that act is not so much that the Germans should think it no crime to shoot a woman, but
that they should be wholly incapable of realizing how
such an atrocious deed would shock the conscience of
the world. They were surprised—think of it!—by the
world's indignation!"

In this remark you may see how far deeper his
reflections take him than what passes for reflection

among the propagandists of hate. Abuse of Germany
never occupied his mind, which was sorrowfully engaged
in striving to comprehend the spiritual conditions of the
German people: he realized, that is to say, that we were
not fighting an enemy who could be shouted down or
made ashamed by abusive epithets, but that we were
opposing a spirit whose anger and temper were entirely different from our own, and therefore a spirit
which must be understood if we were to conquer it. It
was not merely the armies of Germany which must be
defeated, it was the soul of Germany which had to be
converted. He saw this clearly: he never ceased to
work to that end; but he failed to take the nation into
his confidence and the public never understood what he
was after. A fanatic would have left the nation in
no doubt of his purpose.

Every now and then he has half let the nation see
what was in his mind. For example, he has taken
those illuminating, those surely inspired, words of
Edith Cavell as the text for more than one address—
Patriotism is not enough. But beautiful and convincing
as these addresses have been, their spirit has always
had the wistful and *piano* tones of philosophy, never
the consuming fervour of fanaticism. He knows, as
few other men know, that without a League of Nations
the future of civilization is in peril, even the future
of the white races; but he has never made the world
feel genuine alarm for this danger or genuine enthusiasm for the sole means that can avert it. He has not

preached the League of Nations as a way of salvation; he has only recommended it as a legal tribunal.

It is apparently difficult for a politician, however statesmanlike his qualities, to realize that politics cannot be even divorced from morality, much less to comprehend that morality is the very sinew of politics, being in truth nothing more than the conscience of a nation striving to express itself in State action. Because of this politics become degraded and sink to the lowest levels of a mere factional manœuvring for place. They engage the attention of the attorney, and earn nothing but the contempt of the wise. They become like the perversions of art in the hands of those who assert that art has nothing to do with morals; they interest only a handful of experts.

But a man like Lord Robert Cecil does surely apprehend that the essence of politics is morality and, therefore, his unwillingness to use moral weapons in the political arena is hard to understand. He debates where he should appeal; he criticizes where he should denounce; and he accepts a compromise where he should lead a revolt. He is also altogether too civil for the rogues with whom he has to do.

I remember being in the House of Commons on an afternoon when Mr. Lloyd George was expected to make an important speech. Lord Robert Cecil sat in a corner seat on the back benches; his brother, Lord Hugh, occupied the corner seat on the front bench below the gangway. During the Prime Minister's speech, which was a succession of small scoring points against the Labour Party delivered with that spirit of cocksureness which has grown with him in the last few years, I noticed Lord Robert make a pencilled note on a slip of paper and pass it across the gangway with a nod of his head toward Lord Hugh. I watched the journey of this little paper and watched to see its effect. Lord Hugh unfolded the slip of paper, read it, smiled very boyishly all over his face, and, folding it up again, slowly turned his head and looked back towards his brother. The smile they exchanged was a Cecilian biography. One saw in the light of that instant and whole-hearted smile the danger of a keen sense of ironical humour. Both these men have the making of creative fanatics; in both of them there is an intense moral earnestness and in both great intellectual power; but nature has mixed up with these gifts, which were intended for mankind, a drollery of spirit, only amusing in the confidence of private life which they have allowed to weaken their sincerities. Humanity may be thankful that St. Paul was without a sense of humour.

During the war, as Minister of Blockade, Lord Robert Cecil rendered services of the greatest magnitude to his countrymen: he kept Sweden out of the war when the Russian Foreign Office could hardly breathe for anxiety on this point, and at a time when many British newspapers were doing their best to facilitate the great desire of Germany to march an army through

Sweden and Finland to the thus easily reached Russian capital. His work, too, at the Peace Conference in Paris entitles him to the gratitude of the nation: he kept the idea of the League of Nations alive in an atmosphere that was charged with war. He prevented these conferences from making "a Peace to end Peace." But on the whole I feel that he is rather the shadow of great statesmanship leaning diffidently over the shoulder of political brute force than the living spirit of great statesmanship leading the moral conscience of the world away from barbarism towards nobler reason and less partial truth.

MR. WINSTON CHURCHILL

MR. WINSTON CHURCHILL

The Rt. Hon. Winston Churchill (Leonard Spencer) son of Lord Randolph Churchill. Born, 1874. Educ.: Harrow and Sandhurst. Entered army in 1895; served with Spanish Forces in Cuba, 1895; in operations in India, 1897–98; on the Nile and at the Battle of Khartoum, 1899; was given the Khartoum Medal in that year; Correspondent of the *Morning Post* in South Africa, 1899–1900; taken prisoner and escaped, 1900; in long series of actions including Spion Kop, Pieters, and capture of Pretoria; M.P. Oldham, 1900–06; M.P. for Manchester, 1906–08; commissioned Colonel, 1916; retired, 1916; Under Colonial Secretary, 1906–08; President Board of Trade, 1908–10; Home Secretary, 1910–11; First Lord of the Admiralty, 1911–15; Minister of Munitions, 1917; Rector of Aberdeen Univ., 1914; Chairman of the Duchy of Lancaster, 1915; Author of a series of books (campaign records), and also of the *Life of Lord Randolph Churchill.*

RT. HON. WINSTON CHURCHILL

CHAPTER IX

MR. WINSTON CHURCHILL

"He was not free from that careless life-contemning desperation, which sometimes belongs to forcible natures. . . . He was too heedless of his good name and too blind to the truth that though right and wrong may be near neighbours, yet the line that separates them is of an awful sacredness."— JOHN MORLEY (of Danton).

MR. WINSTON CHURCHILL was one of its most interesting figures in the Parliament which included Joseph Chamberlain, Charles Dilke, and George Wyndham. With the fading exception of Mr. Lloyd George, he is easily the most interesting figure in the present House of Commons.

There still clings to his career that element of great promise and unlimited uncertainty which from his first entrance into politics has interested both the public and the House of Commons. He has disappointed his admirers on several occasions, but not yet has he exhausted their patience or destroyed their hopes.

His intellectual gifts are considerable, his personal courage is of a quality that makes itself felt even in the bosom of hate, and he possesses in a unique degree the fighting qualities of the born politician. No man is more difficult to shout down, and no man responds more gratefully to opposition of the fiercer kind. If on several occasions he has disappointed his friends, also on several occasions he has confounded his enemies.

From his youth up Mr. Churchill has loved with all his heart, with all his mind, with all his soul, and with all his strength, three things—war, politics, and himself. He loved war for its dangers, he loves politics for the same reason, and himself he has always loved for the knowledge that his mind is dangerous—dangerous to his enemies, dangerous to his friends, dangerous to himself. I can think of no man I have ever met who would so quickly and so bitterly eat his heart out in Paradise.

He was once asked if politics were more to him than any other pursuit of mankind.

"Politics," he replied, "are almost as exciting as war, and quite as dangerous."

"Even with the new rifle?"

"Well, in war," he answered, "you can only be killed once, but in politics many times."

Unhappily for himself, and perhaps for the nation, since he has many of the qualities of real greatness, Mr. Churchill lacks the unifying spirit of *character* which alone can master the discrepant or even antagonistic elements in a single mind, giving them not merely force, which is something, but direction, which is much more. He is a man of truly brilliant gifts, but you cannot depend upon him. His love for danger runs away with his discretion; his passion for adventure makes

him forget the importance of the goal.   Politics may be
as exciting and as dangerous as war, but in politics
there is no V.C.

I am not enamoured of the logic of consistency.   It
seems a rather ludicrous proceeding for an impecunious
young man to join a very strictly political club with the
idea in his mind that he will always be in favour of that
particular party's programmes.   Most of us, I think,
will agree that a man who never changes his opinion
is a stupid person, and that one who boasts in grave
and hoary age of his lifelong political consistency is
merely confessing that he has learnt nothing in the
school of experience.   One sees the danger of this state
of mind when he thinks of the theologians who burned
men of science at the stake rather than be false to their
Christian dogmas.

Nevertheless, illogical and ridiculous as consistency
may appear, amounting in truth to nothing more than
either inability to see the other side of an argument or a
deliberate refusal to acknowledge an intellectual mistake, who can doubt that this quality of the mind
creates confidence?   On the other hand, who can doubt
that one who appears at this moment fighting on the left
hand, and at the next moment fighting just as con-
vincingly on the right, creates distrust in both armies?

A newspaper which says at one time, "France must
be rolled in mud and blood, her colonies must be taken
from her and given to Germany, she has no sense of
honour"; and at another time describes every German

as a Hun and hails France as the glory of civilization, does not encourage the judicious reader to look for guidance in its editorial pronouncements. But the newspaper which felt itself obliged to offer France a respectful admonition on one occasion and even to oppose French policy with firmness and to express sympathy with the Germans might afterwards acclaim the great virtues of France and oppose itself to the German nation without any loss of our respect. In the one case the inconsistency arises from hysterical and immoral passion, in the other from a moral principle.

There is only one region in which consistency has the great sanction of an indubitable virtue: it is the region of moral character. A good man, a man who makes us feel that righteousness is the breath of his nostrils, may change his intellectual opinions many times without losing our confidence, deeply as we may deplore his change. Goodness has an effect on men's minds which can hardly be exaggerated. Conduct is the one sphere in which consistency has an absolute merit. A man whose whole life is governed by moral principle has a constituency in the judgment of all honest people and may be said to represent mankind rather than a party. Even a cynical opportunist like Lord Beaconsfield had to confess, "So much more than the world imagines is done by personal influence."

Mr. Churchill has not convinced the world of this possession. He carries great guns, but his navigation is uncertain, and the flag he flies is not a symbol which

stirs the blood.   His effect on men is one of interest
and curiosity, not of admiration and loyalty.   His
power is the power of gifts, not character.   Men watch
him, but do not follow him.   He beguiles the reason,
but never warms the emotions.   You may see in him
the wonderful and lightning movements of the brain,
but never the beating of a steadfast heart.   He has
almost every gift of statesmanship, and yet, lacking the
central force of the mind which gives strength and
power to character, these gifts are for ever at the sport
of circumstance.   His inconsistencies assume the
appearance of shifts and dodges.

There is one particular way in which I think his inconsistencies have been dangerous to his career.   They
have brought him too often into inferior company.

Lord Northcliffe, with all his faults, is a man to
whom statesmen may speak their minds without loss of
influence, but there are other newspaper proprietors,
financiers of commercialized journalism, with whom a
man of Mr. Churchill's power and position should hold
no personal relations.   His is a mind which stands
in need of constant communion with men of culture
and refinement.   He knows the world by this time well
enough, what he does not know are the heights.   His
character suffers, I think, from association with second-
rate people.   He is too heedless of his good name.

Is it too late for him to acquire strength of character?
His faults are chiefly the effects of a forcible and impetuous temperament: they may be expected to diminish as

age increases and experience moulds. But character does not emerge out of the ashes of temperament. It is not to be thought that Mr. Churchill is growing a character which will presently emerge and create devotion in his countrymen. Character for him must lie in those very qualities which are now chiefly responsible for his defects—his ardour, his affectibility, his vehemence, his impetuous rashness, his unquestioned courage. One thing only can convert those qualities into terms of character, it is a new direction.

There is perhaps only one other man in the present House of Commons who could do more than Mr. Churchill for his country and the world. All Mr. Churchill needs is the direction in his life of a great idea. He is a Saul on the way to Damascus. Let him swing clean away from that road of destruction and he might well become Paul on his way to immortality. This is to say, that to be saved from himself Mr. Churchill must be carried away by enthusiasm for some great ideal, an ideal so much greater than his own place in politics that he is willing to face death for its triumph, even the many deaths of political life.

At present he is but playing with politics. Even in his most earnest moments he is only "in politics" as a man is "in business." But politics for Mr. Churchill, if they are to make him, if they are to fulfil his promise, must be a religion. They must have nothing to do with Mr. Churchill. They must have everything to do with the salvation of mankind.

It is time, high time, he hitched his waggon to a star.

Ever since I first met him, when he was still in the twenties, Mr. Churchill has seemed to me one of the most pathetic and misunderstood figures in public life.   People have got it into their heads that he is a noisy, shameless, truculent, and pushing person, a sort of intellectual Horatio Bottomley of the upper classes. Nothing could be further from the truth.

Mr. Churchill is one of the most sensitive of prominent politicians, and it is only by the exercise of his remarkable courage that he has mastered this element of nervousness.   Ambition has driven him onward, and courage has carried him through, but more often than the public thinks he has suffered sharply in his progress.   The impediment of speech, which in his very nervous moments would almost make one think his mouth was roofless, would have prevented many men from even attempting to enter public life; it has always been a handicap to Mr. Churchill, but he has never allowed it to stop his way, and I think it is significant both of his courage and the nervousness of his temperament that while at the beginning of a speech this thickness of utterance is most noticeable, the speaker's pale face showing two patches of fiery pink in his cheeks, the utterance becomes almost clear, the face shows no sign of self-consciousness, directly he has established sympathy with his audience.   It is interesting to notice an accent of brutality in his speaking, so different from the suave and charming tones of Mr. Balfour; this accent of brutality, however, is not the note of a brutal character, but of a highly strung temperament fighting its own sensibilities for mastery of its own mind. Mr. Churchill is more often fighting himself than his enemies.

His health has been against him: his heart and his lungs have not given him the support he needs for his adventurous and stormy career. At times, when every man's hand has seemed to be against him, he has had to fight desperately with both body and mind to keep his place in the firing line. Some of his friends have seen him in a state of real weakness, particularly of physical weakness, and for myself I have never once found him in a truculent or self-satisfied frame of mind. I believe he is at heart a modest man, and I am quite certain he is a delicate and a suffering man. But for the devotion of his wife I think he could not have held his place so long.

Fate, too, has opposed him. His enemies are never tired of shouting the two names of Antwerp and Gallipoli. They are convenient terms of abuse: I suppose they would have destroyed most politicians; certainly they are more deadly than such a phrase as "spiritual home," for although the world may be ignorant of the fact, every honest, educated man must acknowledge a debt of gratitude to the thinkers of ancient Germany, while to be associated with operations which involve the suffering, the death, and the defeat of British troops is in every way more fatal to reputation.

But, in truth, both these strokes of military strategy were sound in conception. I doubt indeed if the military historian of the future, with all the documents before him, will not chiefly condemn the Allies for their initial failure to make Antwerp a sea-fed menace to the back of the German Armies; while even in our own day no one doubts that if Lord Kitchener, in one of his obstinate moods, had not refused to send more divisions to Gallipoli we should have taken Constantinople. The fault of those operations lay not in attempting them but in not adequately supporting them.

Mr. Churchill has had bad luck in these matters, but even here it is the lack of character which has served him most ill. He never impressed Lord Kitchener as a man of power, although that sullen temperament grew in the end to feel an amused affection for him. He did excellent work at the Admiralty, work of the highest kind both before and at the outbreak of war, but his colleagues in the Cabinet never realized the importance of this work, judging it merely as "one of Winston's new crazes." Ministers speak of him in their confidences with a certain amount of affection, but never with real respect. Many of them, of course, fear him, for he is a merciless critic, and has an element of something very like cruelty in his nature; but even those who do not fear him, or on the whole rather like him, will never tell you that he is a man to whom they turn in their difficulties, or a man to whom the whole Cabinet looks for inspiration.

General William Booth of the Salvation Army once told Mr. Churchill that he stood in need of "conversion." That old man was a notable judge of character.

LORD HALDANE

LORD HALDANE

The Rt. Hon. Richard Burdon Haldane was born in 1856. Graduate of Edinburgh University; Professor of Philosophy, St. Andrew's University; Barrister, 1879; Q.C., 1890; created 1st Viscount, 1911; M.P. from Haddingtonshire, 1885–1911; Sec'y for War, 1905–12; Rector of Edinburgh Univ.; Chancellor, Univ. of Bristol; Author of various philosophical works.

RT. HON. RICHARD BURDON HALDANE

CHAPTER X

LORD HALDANE

"He is Attic in the sense that he has no bombast, and does not strive after affect, and that he can speak interestingly on many subjects 'without raising his voice.'"—GILBERT MURRAY (on Xenophon).

IF for nothing else, the nation owes Lord Haldane a debt of gratitude for the example he has given it in behaviour. No man so basely deserted by his colleagues and so scandalously traduced by his opponents ever faced the world with a greater calm or a more untroubled smile.

Lessing said of grief in sculpture that it may writhe but it must not scream. Lord Haldane has not even writhed. When a member of the House of Lords asked him what he proposed doing with the two sacks crammed full of abusive letters addressed to him there by correspondents who thus obeyed a vulgar editor's suggestion, Lord Haldane replied with very good humour, "I have an oyster-knife in my kitchen and an excellent scullery-maid in my establishment: I shall see only my personal letters."

In the darkest hour of his martyrdom, when the oldest and staunchest of his political friends maintained an absolute silence, he gave no sign of suffering and uttered no single word either of surprise or bitterness. He seemed to some of us in those days almost wanting in sensibility, almost inhuman in his serenity. Newspaper articles which made most of us either wince or explode with anger did nothing more to the subject of their vilification than to set him off laughing—a comfortable, soft-sounding, and enjoying laughter which brought a light into his face and gently shook his considerable shoulders. He loved to produce at those moments the encomiums pronounced on his work at the War Office by those very newspapers only a few years before at the hour of his triumphant retirement.

This tranquillity of spirit owed nothing to an unimpressionable mind or a thick skin. One came to see that it was actually that miracle of psychology, a philosophic temperament in action. I believe he could have the toothache without a grimace. He has not only studied philosophy, he has become a philosopher, and not merely a philosopher in theory but a philosopher in soul—a practising philosopher. He might stagger for a moment under the shock of a tremendous sorrow to one whom he loved, but not all the shovings of all the halfpenny editors of our commercialized journalism, not even the most contemptible desertion of his friends, could move his equilibrium by a hair's breadth.

After the noble tributes paid to him by Lord Haig and Lord French I need not trouble the reader by dealing with the accusations brought against the greatest of our War Ministers by the gutter-press or by the baser kind of politicians. It is now acknowledged in all circles outside of Bedlam that Lord Haldane prepared a perfect instrument of war which, shot like an arrow from its bow, saved the world from a German victory, and among the intellectual soldiers it is generally held that if France and Russia had been as well prepared to fulfil their engagements as we were to fulfil ours the war would have ended in an almost immediate victory for the Allies. [1]

It will be more instructive to ask how a man who never made an enemy in his life, and for whom many of our greatest men have a deep affection, came of a sudden to be the target of such general and overwhelming abuse. I think I can do something to clear up this mystery.

When he saw that the great conflict was inevitable, Lord Haldane suggested to Mr. Asquith, then acting as War Secretary, that he should go down to the War Office, where he was still well known and very popular with the intellectual generals, and mobilize his own machine for war. The harassed and overburdened Mr. Asquith gratefully accepted this suggestion.

[1] It is well known that Lord Haig regards Lord Haldane as the greatest Secretary of State for War that England ever had; he has expressed his gratitude again and again for the manner in which Lord Haldane organized the military forces of Great Britain for a war on the Continent. Lord French has said: "He got nothing but calumny and abuse; but the reward to such a man does not come in the ordinary way. I had proved the value of his great work and that is all the reward he ever wanted."

Accordingly Lord Haldane went down to the War Office, and knowing that speed was the one thing to save us from a German avalanche, began to mobilize the Expeditionary Force. Some of the generals were alarmed. War was not yet declared. The cost of mobilization ran into millions. Suppose war did not come after all, how were those millions to be met? Lord Haldane brushed aside every consideration of this kind. Mobilization was to be pushed on, cost what it might. He had not studied his Moltke to no profit.

On leaving the War Office that same day, after having mobilized the British Army, he went across to the Foreign Office and was there stopped by a certain soldier who asked him how many divisions he was sending to France. Lord Haldane very naturally rebuked this person for asking such a question, telling him that war was not yet declared and that therefore perhaps no divisions at all would go to France.

Never was a just reproof more fatal to him who administered it.

I believe this soldier went straight off to an important Civil Servant with the sensational news that Lord Haldane was holding back the Expeditionary Force, and afterwards carried the same false news to one of the most violent anti-German publicists in London, a frenzied person who enjoys nevertheless a certain power in Unionist circles. In a few hours it was all over London that the Liberals were going to desert France, that Lord Haldane, a friend of the German

Kaiser, had got back to the War Office, and that he was preventing mobilization.

I am quite willing to believe that the snubbed soldier honestly thought he was spreading a true story: I am sure that the frenzied publicist believed this story with all the lunatic fervour of his utterly untrained and utterly intemperate mind; but what I cannot bring myself to believe for a moment is that the Unionist statesman to whom this story was taken, and who there and then gave orders for a campaign against Lord Haldane, was inspired by any motive less immoral, less cynical, and less disgraceful to a man of honour than a desire for office.

He saw the opportunity of discrediting the Liberal Government through Lord Haldane and took it. The Cabinet was to fall under suspicion because one of its members could be accused of pro-Germanism. Lord Haldane, against whom his friend Lord Morley now brings the sorrowful charge that he was responsible for the war; Lord Haldane, against whom all the German writers have brought charges of stealing their War Office secrets and of defeating their diplomacy, was to be called a pro-German—a man actually doing Germany's work in the British War Office. And this for a Party purpose.

Mr. Arthur Balfour, by nature the most selfish of men and also an intemperate lover of office, would never have stooped to such dishonour; but among the leaders of the Unionist Party there was to be found a man who saw in a lie the opportunity for a Party advantage and took it.

In these matters a statesman need not show himself. A word to one or two newspaper proprietors is sufficient. Nor need he hunt up any arguments. The newspaper reporter will not leave a dust-bin unsearched. One word, nay, the merest hint is sufficient. So stupid, so supine, is the public, that Fleet Street will undertake to destroy a man's reputation in a week or two.

It was in this fashion that Lord Haldane fell.

"You have killed me," says Socrates, "because you thought to escape from giving an account of your lives. But you will be disappointed. There are others to convict you, accusers whom I held back when you knew it not, they will be harsher inasmuch as they are younger, and you will wince the more."

One day the full truth of this scandalous story will be told, and the historian will then pronounce a judgment which will leave an indelible stain on the reputation of some who with a guilty conscience now sun themselves in the prosperity of public approval. Their children will not read that judgment without bitter shame.

I condemn in this matter not only the man who gave the order for calumny and slander to set to work but, first, the friends of Lord Haldane who kept silence, and, second, the democracy of these islands which allowed itself to be deceived and exploited by the lowest kind of newspapers.

Why was Sir Edward Grey silent? He was living in

Lord Haldane's house at the time, and, agonizing over the abhorrent prospect of European slaughter and striving to the point of a nervous collapse to avert this calamity, was devotedly served and strengthened by his host. Why was he silent?

Why was Mr. Asquith silent? He knew that Lord Haldane had delivered the War Office from chaos and had given to this country for the first time in its history a coherent and brilliantly efficient weapon for this very purpose of a war with Germany. He spoke when it was too late. Why did he not speak when the hounds were in full cry?

And why were Mr. Lloyd George and Mr. Winston Churchill silent? Could they not have told the nation that they had grudged Lord Haldane his Army estimates, and that they had even suggested another and less expensive scheme of national defence—a scheme that was actually examined by the War Office experts and condemned?

Let Mr. Lloyd George look back. If he had had his way with the War Office could Germany have been stopped from reaching Paris and seizing the Channel ports? Moreover, if he had had his way, could he himself have hoped to escape hanging on a lamp-post? Is it not true to say that in saving France from an overwhelming and almost immediate destruction the British Expeditionary Force also saved his neck, the neck of Mr. Winston Churchill, and the necks of all the Cabinet? But if this is so, and his own conscience shall be the judge, how is it that he said no word to the nation which might have saved Lord Haldane from martyrdom?

The nation, I think, does not know what it loses in allowing its judgment to be stampeded by unconscionable journalism. Lord Haldane is no political dilettante. Few men in modern times have brought to politics a mind so trained in right thinking, or a spirit so full of that impressive quality, as Morley calls it, the presentiment of the eve: "a feeling of the difficulties and interests that will engage and distract mankind on the morrow." Long ago he foresaw the need in our industrial life of the scientific spirit, and in our democracy of a deeper and more profitable education. "Look at Scotland, the best educated nation; and at Ireland, the worst!" For these things he prepared. Long ago, too, he thought out a better and a complete system of Cabinet government. Long ago he had seen that the enmity between Capital and Labour must be brought to an end and an entirely new relation brought into existence, identifying the prosperity of the one with the other. For this, too, he had a scheme. These things were the chief concern of his life, and only for these things did he remain in politics.

The nation would have been in a healthier condition if Lord Haldane's reasoned policy had been acted upon and Mr. Lloyd George's talent for oratory had been employed to explain that reasoned policy to the less educated sections of the public, instead of used to arouse

an angry opposition to the unreasoned and disconnected reforms of his own conception.

But what a topsy-turvy world! Mr. Lloyd George is "the man who won the war," he who did nothing to prepare for it, and suggested some things that might have made it difficult to be won; while Lord Haldane, who did prepare for it, and whose work did save the whole world, is cast out of office. And when the war is won, and Lord Haldane's position has been publicly and nobly vindicated by Lord Haig, Mr. Lloyd George as Prime Minister of England has a portfolio for Mr. Austen Chamberlain and another for Dr. Macnamara, but none for this man to whom more than to any other politician he owes his place and perhaps his life.

Lord Haldane is not what Prodicus used to call "a Boundary Stone, half philosopher and half practical statesman." His philosophy is his statesmanship, and his statesmanship is his philosophy. He has brought to the study of human life a profound mind and a trained vision. His search after truth has destroyed in him all pettiness of personal ambition. He desires, because he regards it as the highest kind of life, to further the work of creative evolution, to be always on the side of spiritual forces, and never to be deceived by transitory materialism. Democracy has need of these qualities, and a great empire without such qualities in its statesmen can hardly endure the test of time.

His faults are a too generous confidence in the good

sense of democracy and a lack of impassioned energy. He is too much a thinker, too little a warrior. Unhappily he is not an effective speaker, and his writing is not always as clear as his ideas. He is at his best in conversation with men whom he likes.

His activity is enormous, but it is the activity of the scholar. He works far into the night, takes little or no exercise, and avoids "that dance of mimes"—the life of society. By hard reading he keeps himself abreast of knowledge in almost every one of its multitudinous departments and will go a long journey to hear a scientific lecture or to take part in a philosophical discussion. He is the friend of philosophers, theologians, men of science, men of letters, and many a humble working man. He was never privately deserted in the long months of his martyrdom. His charming London house, so refined and so dignified in its simplicity, was the frequent meeting-place of many even in those bad days when the door outside was daubed with paint, the windows broken, and a policeman stood on guard. A few of us wished he took his ill-treatment with a fiercer spirit; but looking back now I think that even the youngest of us perceives that he was unconsciously teaching us by his behaviour one of the noblest lessons to be learned in the school of life.

Let his fate teach democracy that when it has found a leader whom it can trust, it must be prepared to fight for him as well as to follow him. No statesman is safe

from the calumny of newspapers, and no statesman
violently and persistently attacked in a crisis can
depend upon the loyalty of his colleagues. It is not
in our politics as it is in our games.

LORD RHONDDA

LORD RHONDDA OF LLANWERN
(DAVID ALFRED THOMAS MACKWORTH)

First Baron, 1916. Born, in Aberdare, Wales, 1856; died, 1919. Educated with tutors, and later at Caius College, Cambridge; Scholar also, of Jesus; President South Wales Liberal Federation, 1893–97; M.P. for Merthyr, 1888–1910; for Cardiff, 1910; Food Controller, 1917–1919.

LORD RHONDDA

CHAPTER XI

LORD RHONDDA

"Whereof what better witness can ye expect I should produce than one of your own now sitting in Parliament."—MILTON.

IN the *Merry Passages and Jests* of old Sir Nicholas Lestrange record is made of the following witty definition: "Edm. Gurney used to say that a mathematitian is like one that goes to markett to buy an axe to break an egg."

This perhaps had been the fate of Lord Rhondda, for he was by nature of a true mathematical turn, had not the circumstances of his economic life forced him to apply this natural tendency to the practical affairs of commerce. But nature herself had given him with this aptitude for mathematics another quality which must eventually, one would suppose, have saved him from the unfruitful fate of a theorist—he was a man of rare imagination. And so this mathematician, who was also a poet, brought a unique mind to the affairs of commerce and there scored a success which attracted attention in both hemispheres.

I do not know a better example to illustrate the main thesis of this book than the case of Lord Rhondda.   No doubt the case of a greater man, Lord Leverhulme, would lend itself to a far stronger illustration of that thesis, but, unfortunately for my argument and for the nation, Lord Leverhulme has never had an opportunity of vindicating in office those qualities which the House of Commons neglected or overlooked during the years in which, like Lord Rhondda, he sat humbly on its back benches.

For the best part of his manhood Lord Rhondda was a political failure. The House of Commons, which prides itself on its judgment of men, treated him as a person of no importance. He represented one of the largest industrial constituencies in the country, was always returned by an overwhelming majority, and was known to be in his own district an administrator of far-reaching talent; but because he could not speak effectually, and because the House of Commons—that most self-satisfied assembly of mediocrities—did not take to him, he was never offered by his political leaders during all the long years of his patient service even an under-secretaryship.

This was the man who saved the nation from one of its greatest perils during perhaps the most critical period of the war.

As one examines Lord Rhondda's administration of the Ministry of 'Food one discovers an interesting and surely an important fact in the psychology of our public life.

His triumph, which was one of the greatest in the war,

lay almost entirely in the region of personality. For his gravest difficulties were not so much in the office of the Ministry as in the great and grumbling world outside, where toiling men and women stood outside provision shops for hours in the rain and cold only to be told in the vast majority of cases when their turn came that supplies were exhausted for that day.

By the power of his imagination Lord Rhondda saw that the first step towards saving a very perilous situation was to convince this vast world of seething discontent that absolute justice should characterize the administration of his office. To this end, satisfied that those about him were men of devoted zeal and real talent, he set himself to the creation of a public opinion favourable to the discharge of his duties. And by a stroke of inspiration he saw that to achieve this tranquillity of the public mind he must give his own personality to the world. His character must become a public possession. A man, and not an office, must stand for Food Control. The instinct of the Briton for justice and fair play must receive assurance from a moral personality.

Therefore no member of the Government was more accessible, or more ready to be interviewed and photographed, than the Food Controller. It was not vanity, but foreseeing statesmanship, which opened his door to the humblest newspaper reporter who visited the Ministry. His personality—a moral, just, fearless, and confident personality—had to be conveyed to the mind of the public, and every interview he gave to the Press had this important objective for its reason. He saw the morals of an economic situation, and he solved those economics very largely by making a moral impression on the public mind.

The work of his office was carried to victory by Sir William Beveridge, Captain Tallents, Professor Gonner, and other very able men in charge of rationing; but this work must have failed had it not been for public confidence in Lord Rhondda's integrity; and, moreover, Lord Rhondda's character played no small part in firing that work with a zeal and passion which were excelled by no other department of public service. Men not only worked hard for him, they worked for him affectionately.

His choice of Mr. J. H. Clynes was inspired by the same idea. He had heard this labour member speak, and had been impressed by the moral qualities of his oratory; he knew that in choosing him to represent the Food Ministry in the House of Commons he might be sure of the confidence of Labour, both there and in the circles of trade unionism. He was not deceived. Mr. Clynes was the most loyal and impressive of lieutenants, who, on one occasion in particular, saved a difficult situation.

Lord Rhondda realized the moral qualities of statesmanship. He appealed to the highest instincts of his countrymen. This was his greatest achievement.

He was in many ways a lovable man. The quality

which chiefly drew people to him was his extreme
boyishness. The remarkable beauty of his face always
seemed to me an expression of this delightful boyishness—his smile deepening this effect in a most charming
manner. He loved life with a boy's fervour, regarding
it always as an opportunity for winning success. The
difficulties of work, like the difficulties of a mathematical problem called out the athletic qualities of an otherwise shy and almost effeminate nature. He loved to pit
his brains against other men, rejoiced to discover
obstacles in his path, never despaired when things went
against him, and infinitely preferred the battle for
success to the success itself. In this, too, he was a boy;
he had to win a fight fairly and honourably to enjoy
the victory. I believe him to have been one of the
most honest and straightforward men that ever made
a fortune in business.

There was no man less embittered by failure and
disappointment. He seems to have had reason to
believe that Mr. Lloyd George frustrated his early
efforts as a politican, indeed he told me more than once
that Mr. Lloyd George had deliberately set himself
to that end; and yet it was at Mr. Lloyd George's
earnest beseeching that he accepted the office of Food
Controller, and once a member of his Cabinet, he seldom
spoke of this old opponent without the warmest
admiration. "You can't trust him a yard," he said to
me on one occasion laughing very good-naturedly; "but
there is not a man in the Government who can hold a

9

candle to him for courage and inspiration. I know very well that I could never have done what he has done. More than any man in the country he has pulled us through the critical days of the war. He is wonderful—nothing short of wonderful—and sometimes I feel almost fond of him, for he has many likeable sides to his character; all the same, I know very well he is not to be trusted. I took office on certain conditions, not one of which has he observed. He is one of those men with whom you cannot deal confidently."

This was the bitterest thing I ever heard him say of his former enemy. As regards the old days in the House of Commons, he told me that there was room for only one leader in Wales, and that, while Mr. Lloyd George could speak, he couldn't, and so Mr. Lloyd George, who was consumed by personal ambition, had won the battle. In saying this he smiled like a boy, and only grew serious when he added of those wasted years, "The bother is I had a lot of useful things I wanted to do for the country."

He was convinced that he could have paid off the whole of the National Debt during those years.

A good judge of statesmen said of Lord Rhondda that he would have made the greatest Chancellor of the Exchequer these islands had ever possessed. I do not think there can be any doubt of this, for his genius lay in figures and he had extraordinary swiftness in seeing his way through expensive chaos to economical order. His mind was constructive, if not positively creative. He was never happier—except when birds'-nesting or romping with young people—than when he was in an arm-chair working out with pencil and paper some problem of administration which involved enormous figures. He would sit up to the small hours of the morning over his work, and would come down to breakfast radiant with happiness, bursting with energy, exclaiming, "I had a glorious time last night!" Certainly he would have brought to the Treasury an original mind, and a mind, moreover, profoundly acquainted with the activities of trade and commerce—those important factors in national finance which appear to cut so small a figure in the minds of bankers and officials.

Although a rather dull speaker, few men of my acquaintance were more lucid and convincing in conversation, particularly when he addressed a sympathetic mind. This was notably the case when he was unfolding his ideas on the conflicting theories of Individualism and Socialism. If his conversations on this head could be printed in a book they would make difficult work even for the most ingenious apologists of Socialism. He was persuaded that no theory of Socialism could be put into successful practice without involving the loss of personal freedom, and that without Individualism there would be no initiative, no audacity, and no creative energy in the development of an industry. Whenever he was in conflict with Socialists he would say to them, "Why don't you buy me out and run the mines yourselves? You have plenty of money in your unions, and I am quite willing to sell."

There were several strange and interesting movements in his otherwise quite simple and boyish nature. For example, he had no religious faith worth speaking about, certainly no dogmatic faith of any kind; but he always said his prayers. Then he held the theory that old age was a form of disease, and so avoided, as much as possible, the society of old people, fearing contagion; the young people with whom he loved to surround himself, and on whom he delighted to play many practical jokes, he called his "young germs."

He was entirely free from all forms of snobbishness, and would make fun of titles and honours and ridicule aristocratic pretensions; yet he went somewhat painfully out of his way to get a title from his Party when he retired from the House of Commons, and was justly indignant at the way this bargain was broken by the Liberal leaders of that day. I think he wanted a title at that time chiefly to prove to his constituents that he had faithfully done his duty by them.

He seldom read a book of any account after he came down from Cambridge, but hardly a day of his life passed that he did not learn by heart a number of fine sayings which appealed to him in a book of quotations. These quotations he would fire off at his family till they cried for mercy, or another set.

He was far happier among his Herefords at Llanwern than in London or in Cardiff, but he was for ever postponing the day of his retirement from public life. He kept all his boy's love for birds and animals, and had real feeling for beautiful things in nature; but the game of life drew him always towards the city.

At one time he smoked a prodigious number of cigars and drank a bottle of port every night, but about twenty years before his death he gave up both habits on the challenge of a friend and never reverted to them again. Mr. William Brace, the miners' leader, said to me one day, "Rhondda has the income of a duke and the tastes of a peasant, whereas I have the income of a peasant and the tastes of a duke." I told Lord Rhondda this, and he smiled quietly over the remark, saying, "He's a very pleasant fellow, Brace: fond of pictures, and a good judge of them, too. Yes, I suppose my tastes are rather simple when you come to look at them, but I don't find them cheap." He was on excellent terms with Labour politicians, knew many of the old miners with real intimacy, and could handle large bodies of men with consummate tact.

I do not think for a moment that he was a very great man, but I can think of few Cabinet ministers during the last thirty years who were anything like so well-fitted to render the nation real and lasting service. Lord Rhondda had genius, and though a boyish egoist in his private life he was earnestly and most eagerly anxious to sacrifice all he possessed for the good of the

State. That he came so late and for so brief a period to power I regard, if not as a national misfortune, at any rate as a striking condemnation of our methods of government.

LORD INVERFORTH

LORD INVERFORTH
1ST BARON OF SOUTHGATE
(ANDREW WEIR)

Born, 1865. Head of firm of Andrew Weir and Co. shipowners of
Glasgow, Surveyor General of Supplies, 1917–19; Minister of Munitions,
1919.

By permission of Russell & Sons

LORD INVERFORTH

CHAPTER XII

LORD INVERFORTH

"Gratitude is a fruit of great cultivation; you do not find it among gross people."—Dr. Johnson.

We are keeping up Voltaire's idea of our English character. Instead of only admirals, however, we are now hanging all sorts and descriptions of our public servants, but whether to encourage the others or to pay off a grudge, who shall determine?

Lord Inverforth takes his hanging very well. One might go so far as to say that he is not merely unaware of the noose round his neck but so perverse as to think he is still alive. His sense of humour is as good to him as a philosophic temperament.

I like his sense of humour. It manifests itself very quietly and with a flash of unexpectedness. One day at luncheon he was speaking of Lord Leverhulme, whose acquaintance he had made only a week or two before. Someone at the table said, "What I like about Leverhulme is his simplicity. In spite of all his tremendous undertakings he preserves the heart of a boy." With a twinkle in his eyes, and in a soft inquiring voice, "Have you ever tried to buy glycerine from him?" asked Lord Inverforth.

This story has a sequel. I mentioned it to Lord Leverhulme. "One day two Englishmen," he replied at once, "were passing the Ministry of Munitions. They saw Lord Inverforth going in. One who did not recognize him said, 'Anyone can tell that man; he's a Scotsman.' To which the other, who did recognize him, replied, 'Yes, but you couldn't tell *that* Scotsman anything else.' You might repeat that story to Lord Inverforth the next time you meet him."

I did, and the Minister of Munitions accepted the compliment with a good grace.

It is a fortunate thing for this country that a man of so remarkable a genius for organization as Lord Inverforth should be found willing to serve the national interests in spite of an almost daily campaign of abuse directed against his administration. I sometimes wish he would bring an action for libel against one of these critics. It would be an amusing case. He might claim damages of, let us say, £7,000,000 or even £10,000,000, for he is a man of gigantic interests, claiming these damages on the score that his alleged libellers have injured his reputation as a man of business in all quarters of the world. They would have him the craziest muddler and the most easily swindled imbecile outside Fleet Street—where alone wisdom is to be found. How one would enjoy a verbatim report of the cross-examination of these critics *in their own newspapers*.

I will endeavour to show that Lord Inverforth is not quite so consummate an ass as his critics would have the public to believe, but rather one of the very greatest men, in his own particular line, who ever came to the rescue of a chaotic Government.

Let me not be supposed to insist that a great man of business is a great man. I regard Lord Inverforth as an exceedingly great man of business, one of the very greatest in the world, and this fact I hope to make clear in a few lines, but I do not regard him as a national hero in the wider sense of that term. He has too many lacks for that, and some of them essential to true and catholic greatness.

He could never fire the imagination of a people, nor does he convey a warm and generous feeling to the heart. His enthusiasms are all of a subdued nature. The driving force in his character which has made him so powerful a man of business, owes little to the higher virtues. He has found the plain of life too full of absorbing interest and too crowded with abounding opportunities for getting on to raise his eyes to the mountains. This is not to say that he is a man of no ideals, but to say that his ideals are of too practical and prosaic a kind ever to stir the pulses with excitement.

Nevertheless I regard him as a born statesman, and could wish that the conditions of political life made it more easy for a man of his gifts to serve the country than men with the gifts of, let us say, Dr. Macnamara or Sir Hamar Greenwood.

The world knows so little of him that perhaps I may begin my political reflections in this case with a brief summary of his career, such details of a business man's biography as may contribute to an understanding of his character.

Andrew Weir, as he was in those days, went to school at Kirkcaldy, where he was chiefly notable for seeking information on more subjects than came under the jurisdiction of his pedagogue's ferule. A benign Rosa Dartle might have been his godmother. He was for ever consulting encyclopædias and books of reference. However badly he knew his Greek verbs or his Latin syntax he had a very shrewd and curious knowledge of the world when he left school at fifteen to enter the local branch of the Commercial Bank of Scotland.

At school he had wanted to own ships. This ambition still lodged in his brain. His thoughts were all at sea. There was no romance in the world so pleasing to his soul as the romance of the merchant marine. He had a real passion for harbours. He loved the idea of far voyages. The smells of cargoes and warehouses composed a sea-bouquet for him which he esteemed sweeter than all the scents of hedges and wood. If there was a big man for him in the world it was the sailor.

I don't think he had so profound a feeling for bankers. Not quite so downright as Lord Leverhulme in stating his opinion of bankers, Lord Inverforth nevertheless regards them on the whole as lacking in courage and imagination. He said to himself on his banker's stool, "I will learn all I can, but I won't stay here; I'll be a shipowner."

In his twentieth year he bought a sailing ship. This was at Glasgow in the year 1885. He called himself Andrew Weir and Co. He had the feeling that sailing ships, engaged in coastwise trade, might be bigger. He announced his intention of building a large coasting ship. People informed him, with an almost evangelical anxiety as to his commercial salvation, that he was a lunatic. But the big ship was a success. He built more and bigger. Then, in 1896 he said to himself, "Why shouldn't steam be used in the coasting trade?" and he went into steam. Again there were inquiries after his mental health, but the steamer flourished like the big sailing ship. At the beginning of what the curate called "this so-called twentieth century" the firm of Andrew Weir and Co. flew its flag in all the ports under heaven, and controlled the largest fleet of sailing ships in the world.

There is this fact to be noticed in particular. Mr. Andrew Weir's inquisitive mind had not merely mastered the grammar of shipowning but had crammed the cells of his brain with the whole encyclopædia of commercial geography. He knew each season what the least of the islands of the world was producing, and the crops, manufactures, and financial condition of every country across the sea. He knew, also, the way in which the various nations conducted the business of transport. From his office in Glasgow he could see the whole vast labours of industrious and mercantile man, that Brobdingnagian ant of this revolving globe, merely by closing his eyes. The map of the world's commerce was cinematographed upon his brain.

One thing more remains to be said. Mr. Andrew Weir inherited the moral traditions of Scotch industry. He grew rich, but not ostentatious. His increasing fortune went back and back into trade. He never dreamed either of cutting a figure in plutocratic society or making himself a public character. A quiet, rather shy, and not often articulate person, he lived a frugal life, loving his business because it occupied all his time and satisfied nearly every curiosity of his inquiring mind.

War came, and Mr. Weir was busier than ever with his ships. Not until 1917 did it occur to the Government that the work of buying supplies for its gigantic armies was something only to be mastered by a man of business. The nation may be grateful to Mr. Lloyd George for having discovered in Glasgow perhaps the one man in the British Isles who knew everything there was to know about commercial geography.

Mr. Andrew Weir entered the War Office in March, 1917, as Surveyor General of Supply. The position was not merely difficult in its nature, but difficult in its circumstances. Soldiers are jealous animals, and not easily does the War Office take to the black-coated man of business. Mr. Weir was tact itself. For some weeks the soldiers were hardly aware of his presence, then they learned that the quiet Scotsman in the black coat was saying the most laudatory things about their organization; then they found themselves marvellously improving this organization merely by acting on the most modestly given suggestions from the smooth civilian; and finally the very greatest of them discovered that somehow or another Supply had now got a wonderful "move on," and that among other things this wonderful "move on" had brought the civilian on top of them—still smooth and modest, still in the background, but absolute master of the whole machinery.

Lord Inverforth's work soon involved not merely the care of the British Armies but the care of the Allied nations. What did he do? Besieged by the unconscionable rascals of the world, fawning or blustering to get contracts at extraordinary prices, Lord Inverforth struck a master blow at this international cupidity by obtaining control of the principal raw materials and instituting the system of costing. Manufacturers got their contracts on a fixed basis of profits. Lord Inverforth knew the exact cost of every stage in the manufacture of each article he bought, and he saw that the manufacturer received from the taxpayer only a small percentage of profit on that cost.

The greatest thing he did at that time, and the bravest, for he did it without authorization and at a cost of £250,000,000, was to buy up the Australasian wool-clip from 1917 to 1920. In this way Germany was doomed to defeat. England, so to speak, had the clothing of humanity in her right hand.

But Lord Inverforth also controlled flax, hemp, leather, and jute, so that the enemy's case was as hopeless as our own was secure.

These gigantic operations involved an expenditure of over £500,000,000. They brought an actual profit to the British Government of over £20,000,000, saved the taxpayer Heaven only knows how many millions, and were conducted at an administrative cost of three shillings for every £100.

Nothing like it had ever been done before in the world.

Early in 1919 Lord Inverforth was asked to clear up war's rubbish-heap. He became Minister of Munitions. Within twenty-four hours his body of expert buyers had become the Disposal Board—a body of expert sellers.

The property of the British taxpayer was scattered over four continents, and in all manner of places in those four continents. It was composed of 350,000 different kinds of things.

At once Lord Inverforth was again besieged by the rascals. There was an army of them, composed of many "rings," seeking to buy up these "waste products of war" at a knock-down price. At the same time came the blustering contractor, cheated by peace of his contract, with a claim for millions on one ground or another.

Lord Inverforth made it clear, first, that the stores were to be sold at a commercial value, and, second, that he would protect the taxpayer against extortionate claims on the part of contractors. As regards this second difficulty, pressure was brought against him from the very highest political quarters to admit certain claims and to avoid legal action. His reply was, "I will resign before I initial those claims."

He fought them all, and he beat them all. He saved the taxpayer millions of pounds.

As for the disposal of stores, he has already brought to the Exchequer over £500,000,000, and before these pages are printed that sum may be increased to something like £800,000,000.

The least imaginative reader will perceive from this brief statement that a veritable Napoleon of Commerce ¹ ᴊs presided over the business side of the war. Where there was every opportunity for colossal waste, there has been the most scientific economy; where there was every likelihood of wholesale corruption, there has been an unsleeping vigilance of honesty; and where, at the end, there might have been a tired carelessness resulting in ruinous loss, there has been up to the very last moment an unremitting enthusiasm for the taxpayers' interest which has resulted in a credit contribution to the national balance sheet of £800,000,000.

I have left to the last this not unworthy feature of Lord Inverforth's labours. Those labours have been given to the nation. He, at the head of things, and the chiefs of the Disposal Board under him, have refused to accept any financial reward. One and all

10

they deserted their businesses and slaved from morning to night in the national interests, and one and all they gave their services to the State.

What has been Lord Inverforth's reward from the public? From first to last he has been attacked by a considerable section of the Press, and has been accused in Parliament of incredible waste and incorrigible stupidity. Let it be supposed (I do not grant it for a moment) that he made mistakes, even very great mistakes, still, on the total result of his gigantic labours, does not the public owe him a debt of gratitude? Has he not been an honest man at the head of a department where dishonesty had its chief opportunity? Did he not strike a death blow at Germany when he secured, with a suddenness which ruined his rivals in the field, the wool-clip of the world? Is there one man in these islands who thought for a moment that the overplus of stores would fetch a sum of £800,000,000?

I will say a word about Slough, which is still the favourite cry of Lord Inverforth's critics, who have held their peace about the "dumps" since the publication of the White Paper describing the sale of stores.

Slough was the work of the War Office. It was begun badly. Mistakes of a serious kind were made. It might have been a financial disaster. But Lord Inverforth is a chivalrous man. He has never disclosed the fact that he inherited Slough. In the face of violent criticism he has maintained a dignified silence, letting the world think that he was the parent of the

idea, and bending all his energies to make it a success.
He has had his reward.   Slough has been sold and the
transaction shows a profit for the taxpayer.

During the last years of his administration I saw a
good deal of Lord Inverforth.   He was anxious to get
back to his own work.   He asked again and again to be
relieved of his duties—the machinery he had set up
being in excellent running order.   But the Prime
Minister begged him to stay, and he has stayed, against
his will and against his own interests, and all the time
he has been subjected to a stream of malignant criticism.

Let the reader ask himself whether the case of Lord
Inverforth is likely to encourage the best brains in the
country to come to the political service of the nation.
Is there not a danger that we may fall into the American
position, and have our great men in commerce and our
second-rate men in politics?

I regard Lord Inverforth as one of the few very great
men in commerce who have the qualities of genuine
statesmanship.   I am not at liberty to give my chief
grounds for this belief, but before long the world may
know from Lord Inverforth's commercial activities on
the Continent that more than any other man in these
islands he has seen the way and taken the step to
reconstruct the shattered civilization of Europe.

On many occasions I have discussed with him the
future of mankind.   I have found him the least anxious
and always the most self-possessed observer of events.
Quiet, patient, practical, and imaginative, inspired too

by humane motives, he cherishes the unshakable faith that Great Britain is destined to lead civilization into the future as far as human eye can see. He places his faith in British character. Rivalry on the part of powerful nations, even when it is directed against our key industries, does not disturb him in the least. While others are crying, "How shall we save ourselves?" he is pushing the fortunes of the British race in every quarter of the world. And where British trade goes, on the whole there goes too the highest civilizing power in the world—British character. It is significant of his faith that he has ever worked to get the British mercantile marine manned by men of the British race, and to this end has led the way in improving the conditions of the British seaman's life.

"All the fallacies and wild theories of revolutionary minds," he once said to me, "break ultimately on the rock of industrial fact. The more freely nations trade together the more clearly will it be seen that humanity must work out its salvation within the limits of economic law. And the way to a smooth working out of that salvation is by recognizing the claims of the moral law. We are men before we are merchants. There is no reason why mistrust should exist between management and labour. The economic law by no means excludes, but rather demands, humaneness. I believe that a system of profit sharing can be devised which will bring management and labour into a sensible partnership. Selfishness on the part of capital is as bad as selfishness on the part of labour. Both must be unselfish, both must think of the general community, and ooth must work hard. The two chief enemies of mankind are moral slackness and physical slackness."

There is no man living who would make a better Chancellor of the Exchequer than this merchant prince who, however, has had enough of politics and is going back very gladly to his desk in the City. He is not in the least soured by the public ingratitude, and rightly judges it to be rather the voice of unscrupulous and stunt-seeking journalism than the considered judgment of the nation. But he has a very poor opinion of the way in which the Government of the country conducts its business.

LORD LEVERHULME

LORD LEVERHULME, 1ST BARON
(WILLIAM HESKETH LEVER)

Born 1851, Lancashire.   Educ.: Bolton Church Institute; Chairman
of Lever Bros., Port Sunlight; High Sheriff, Lancaster, 1917.

LORD LEVERHULME

CHAPTER XIII

LORD LEVERHULME

"Dullness is so much stronger than genius because there is so much more of it, and it is better organized and more naturally cohesive inter se. *So the Arctic volcano can do nothing against Arctic ice."*—SAMUEL BUTLER.

THE reader may properly wonder to find the figure of Lord Leverhulme brought before the mirrors of Downing Street.

But let me explain why I introduce this industrial Triton into the society of our political minnows.

Lord Leverhulme rejected politics only when politics rejected him. He is of that distinguished company to whom the House of Commons has turned both a deaf ear and a cold shoulder. He failed where Mr. Walter Long succeeded, and fell where Dr. Macnamara rose.

I once asked a Cabinet Minister how it was that a man of such conspicuous quality had failed to win office. "I really cannot tell you," he replied with complacency, "but I remember very well that the House of Commons never took to him. It is curious how many men who do well outside the House of Commons fail to make good inside."

Curious indeed! But more curious still, we may surely say, that the House of Commons should continue, in the light of this knowledge, to enjoy so good an opinion of itself.

I suppose that nobody will now dispute that Lord Leverhulme is easily the foremost industrialist, not merely in the British Isles, but in the world. I can think of no one who approaches him in the creative faculty. Not even America, the country of big men and big businesses, has produced a man of this truly colossal stature. Mr. Rockefeller is a name for a committee. Mr. Carnegie was pushed to fortune by his more resolute henchmen. But Lord Leverhulme, as is very well known in America, has been the sole architect of his tremendous fortunes, and in all his numerous undertakings exercises the power of an unquestioned autocrat.

Mr. Lloyd George once remarked to me that the trouble with Lord Leverhulme is that he cannot work with other men. But this is only true in part. Lord Leverhulme can work very well with men who are not fools. When I told him of Mr. Lloyd George's remark, "Well, I don't know," he replied, "I have been working with other men all my life!" Yes, but this, too, expresses only part of the truth. He has been working with these other men as an accepted master.

It is not so in politics. There a man of power cannot pick and choose his colleagues. He must work with fools as well as men of ability. And never can he work as a master. Always at the Cabinet table he will find a cabal of deadheads opposed to the exercise of

his authority, and in the department over which he is
set to rule a bunch of traditional Barnacles, without
one spark of imagination between them, who will fight
his new ideas at every turn.

The essence of politics and government is mediocrity.
The good sense of the House of Commons is a con-
spiracy to resist genius and to enthrone the average
man.   A department of the State is well governed only
when its chief Civil Servant, by the grace of God,
chances to be a man of statesmanlike capacity.

Like Lord Rhondda, Lord Leverhulme was approached by the Government during the numerous
crises of the war to render service to the State.   His
experience in this respect confirmed his judgment that
our system of government is a chaos which would
hardly be tolerated in a business establishment of the
second class.   I will give an incident.

It was a matter of grave urgency to the Government
that margarine should be manufactured in this country.
A Cabinet Minister begged Lord Leverhulme, on the
score of patriotism, to set up such a factory.   Lord
Leverhulme expressed his willingness to take up the
project, but said that he must go to the public for a
certain sum of money to carry it out.   The Cabinet
Minister made no demur to this very natural proposal,
but suggested that it might be well if Lord Leverhulme
would call at the Treasury and inform them of his
purpose.

Accordingly the great industrialist, able as was no

other man in this particular to serve his country's need, called humbly at the Treasury for permission to ask the public for capital. He was received by an official who refused point-blank to listen to such a proposition. Lord Leverhulme mentioned again the name of the Cabinet Minister who had requested him to embark on this venture. This was nothing to the official. He had nothing to do with other departments. His business was to see that the public's money came to the Treasury; he was certainly not going to countenance the raising of money for an industrial purpose.

You could no more have got into this gentleman's head than you could have got into the head of a rabbit the idea that money invested in an essential industrial undertaking pays the State far better than money advanced to it at the cost of five per cent.

Not to weary the reader with an incident, however telling, the end of this affair was that after going backwards and forwards between a Cabinet Minister and a Treasury official, Lord Leverhulme was at last permitted to ask the public for a small sum of money which he himself considered inadequate for the Government's purpose.

I have never heard him speak bitterly of his political experiences, but I have never heard him express anything but an amused contempt for the antiquated machinery which passes amongst politicians for a system of government.

The English [he says] have pushed their fortunes, never by the aid of Government, but on the contrary almost always in the teeth of Government opposition. There is no man so lacking in imagination as a Government official, and no man, unless it is a banker, so wanting in courage as a Cabinet Minister. The wealth of England is the creation of her industrial population. The brains, the faith, the energy of the capitalist, and the brains, the loyalty, the strength of labour, these have made us the first nation of the world. There has been only one real obstacle in our path. Not foreign competition, for that is an incentive, but the cowardice and stupidity of Governments. We possess an empire unrivalled in its opportunities for trade and commerce, an empire which, you would surely think, could not fail to inspire a statesman with great ideas. But what happens? We have a Government which thinks it has exhausted statesmanship by crippling industry at home in order to pay off our war debt as quickly as possible. Instead of setting itself to create more wealth, with the wealth of the world lying at its feet, it sets itself to dry up the sources of wealth at the centre of the empire. But it is no use talking. One thing a Government in this country cannot stand is imagination; and another is courage. The British Empire is in the hands of a lot of clerks—and timid clerks at that. We must do our best to get along without statesmanship at the head.

The reader may not remember that some years before Mr. Lloyd George plunged into a disordered series of social reforms, Lord Leverhulme, sitting in the House of Commons, introduced Bills of a reasonable and connected character to ensure workmen against unemployment and to set up a system of old age pensions. He did not enter Parliament for his own glorification. He had nothing to gain, but much to lose, by devoting himself to the business of Westminster. But he believed that he could benefit the State as a legislator, and he entered Parliament with the definite intention of introducing order into what was self-evidently a condition of dangerous chaos. He had a remedy for slums, a remedy for unemployment, a remedy for the poverty of the workman in old age, and a remedy for the educational deadlock. Further, he cherished the hope that he might do something towards developing the wealth and power of the British Empire, without impairing the spirit of individualism which, in his faith, is the driving power of British fortune.

How many men who entered the House of Commons with no ideas at all have been taken to the friendly bosom of that assembly? Moreover, can the reader name with confidence one Cabinet Minister in the past twenty years who can fairly be compared in creative genius with this remarkable man to whom the House of Commons refused the least of its rewards?

I saw Lord Leverhulme on several occasions at the end of the war. He spoke to me with great freedom of his ideas in the hope that I might carry them with effect to the Prime Minister. He proved to me that it was the nonsense of a schoolboy to talk of making Germany pay for the war, and suggested that the Prime Minister's main appeal to the nation at the General Election of 1918 should be a moral appeal for unity in the industrial world. He had one master word for that great moment in our history. It was the word "Production."

I found this word unpopular in Downing Street. Mr. Lloyd George was more mindful of Lord Northcliffe than of one "who cannot work with other men." And so the word went forth to the British peoples: Germany must pay for the war and the Kaiser must be tried. At the eleventh hour before the election there was no equivocation. Germany *should* pay for the war. The Kaiser *should* be tried. Instead of a great moral appeal, which might have prevented all the disastrous conflicts in industry, and might have preserved the spirit of loyalty which had united the people during the war, the Prime Minister put himself at the head of a disreputable mob calling for revenge.

"One disadvantage of the democratic system," says Mr. Birrell, "is that a Prime Minister no longer feels himself responsible for good government. He awaits a 'mandate' from a mob who are watching a football match."

We have only to compare this order of mind with a mind like Lord Leverhulme's to perceive how it is that politics in our country tend more and more in the American direction. The big men are outside. Politics are little more than a platform for a pugilistic kind of rhetoric. He who can talk glibly and with occasional touches of such sentimentalism as one finds in a Penny Reciter is assured of the ear of the House of Commons, and may fairly count on one day becoming a Minister of

State. But the field for the constructive, imaginative, and creative minds is the field of commerce.

The danger of the State from this condition of things is, unhappily, not only the loss of creative statesmanship at the head of the nation—serious as that is. The danger is greater. Small men are more likely to fall into dishonest ways than big men. There lies, I think, our greatest danger. It seems to me, observing our public life with some degree of intimacy, that there is a growing tendency for the gentleman to fall out of the political ranks and for his place to be filled by the professional politician, who in many cases appears to be almost entirely without moral principle. What can become of such a movement save eventual corruption? At present our politics are stupid but fairly honest. There are still representatives of the old school in the House of Commons. But the conquering advance is from the ranks of professionalism.

I would not have the reader to suppose that I consider Lord Leverhulme a heaven-sent genius of statesmanship. The British constitution is twelve men in a box, and the very spirit of that arrangement is distrust of the expert. Moreover, there is wisdom in the Eastern legend which says that in making genius the fairies left out one essential gift—the knowledge of when to stop.

Whether Lord Leverhulme would have made a better statesman than, let us say, Sir Henry Campbell Bannerman or Mr. Bonar Law it is surely certain, I think, that a true statesman would have made every conceivable use of his unusual mind. This, as I look at things, is the ideal method of government. I do not believe in the business man as statesman. I believe in the trained, cultured, and incorruptible gentleman as statesman, and the business man as his adviser.

But until our politics are of a higher order we can hardly expect the best minds in the nation to feel any attraction to a political career. More and more the professional politician, the narrow man, the man of the loud voice and the one idea, the man who has few instincts of honesty in his mind and no movement of high and disinterested patriotism in his soul, will press himself upon the attention of democracy and by intimidating his leaders and brow-beating his opponents force his way onward to office.

The consideration of this grave peril to the moral character of our public life brings me to my brief conclusion.

CONCLUSION

CHAPTER XIV

CONCLUSION

"While the advances made by objective science and its industrial appli-cations are palpable and undeniable all around us, it is a matter of doubt and dispute if our social and moral advance towards happiness and virtue has been great or any."—MARK PATTISON.

AFTER all, a nation gets the politics that it deserves. The fault is not in our stars, but in ourselves, that we are underlings. If the tone of public life is a low one it is because the tone of society is not a high one. The remedy, then, is not "Sack the lot," but rather, "Repent, lest a worse thing befall thee."

It seems to me that a beginning in moral and social reformation might be made if aristocracy could be encouraged to affirm its ancient rights by the perform-ance of its inherent duties.

We are a nation without standards, kept in health rather by memories which are fading than by examples which are compelling. We still march to the dying music of great traditions but there is no captain of civilization at the head of our ranks. We have indeed almost ceased to be an army marching with confidence towards the enemy, and have become a mob breaking im-patiently loose from the discipline and ideals of our past.

Aristocracy, it must be boldly said, has played

165

traitor to England. It has ceased to lead, and not because it has been thrust from its rightful place by the rude hand of democracy, but because it has deliberately preferred the company of the vulgar. No one has pulled it down, it has itself descended. It has lost its respect for learning, it has grown careless of manners, it has abandoned faith in its duty, it is conscious of no solemn obligations, it takes no interest in art, it is indifferent to science, it is sick of effort, it has surrendered gladly and gratefully to the materialism of plutocracy.

If it could have lost itself in plutocracy the harm would not have been so great; but it still remains for the multitude a true aristocracy, and looking up to that aristocracy for its standards—an aristocracy whose private life is now public property—the multitude has become materialistic, throwing Puritanism to the dogs, and pushing as heartily forward to the trough as any full-fed glutton in the middle or the upper ranks of life.

The standards set by the privileged classes at this time are the same standards as ruled in France before the Revolution. There is no example of modesty, earnestness, restraint, thrift, duty, or culture. Everything is sensual and ostentatious, and shamefacedly sensual and ostentatious.

It is time for the best people in aristocracy to set their faces against this wanton and destructive spirit. It is time a halt was called to luxury and profligacy; time that the door was shut in the face of invading vulgarity. Creation has not agonized in bloody sweat through countless ages of suffering and achievement that those who possess the highest opportunities for doing good should pervert those opportunities into a mere platform for the display of a harmful badness. Evolution was not aiming at Belgravia when it set out on its long journey from the flaming mist of the nebula. We cannot suppose that Nature is content with the egoism of the social butterfly. The very blood of dead humanity cries out for a higher creature.

Aristocracy, one sees, is too apt to regard itself as the spoilt child of material fortune, instead of humbly and with a sense of deepest responsibility accepting the heavy duties of moral leadership imposed upon it by the labours of evolution.

It is to be hoped that the children of the present generation of aristocracy may grow up with no taste for the betting ring, the card room, and the night club, or, at any rate, that a certain number of them may find their highest happiness in knowledge and wisdom rather than in amateur theatricals and fancy-dress balls. The human mind, after all, cannot find rest in triviality, and after so long a period of the most sordid and vulgar self-indulgence it is reasonable to hope that our aristocracy may experience a reaction.

If men would ask themselves, before they rush out to seek her, What is Pleasure? and consult the past history of humanity as well as their own senses and inclinations they could hardly fail, except in the case of the most degenerate, to discover that the highest happiness is not of the nursery or the kitchen, but rather of the living spirit.

Observation of nature, love of beautiful things, delight in noble literature, gratitude for the highest forms of wit and humour, sympathy with all sorts and conditions of men, reverence for the majesty of the universe, kindness to all, love of children, and devotion to the home, these operations of the human spirit bring peace to the heart of man and continue their ministrations to his happiness with an increasing power of joy as his personality enlarges itself to receive the highest revelations of Life.

Something far greater than she is now doing might be done by the Church to restore the sanctions which once ruled human conduct and gave a living force to public opinion. Religion in these days is obviously too complaisant. To watch the Church in the world is to be reminded of a poor relation from the provinces sitting silent and overawed in the gilded drawing-room of a parvenu. There is no sound of confidence in her voice. She whines for the world's notice instead of denouncing its very obvious sins. She is too much in this world, and too little in the other. She is too careful not to offend Dives, and too self-conscious to be seen openly in the company of Lazarus. It is impossible not to think that a coarse world has shaken her faith in Christian virtue. She clings to her traditions and her doctrines, but she has lost the vigorous faith in spiritual life

which gave beauty to those traditions and has ceased
to set that example of entire self-sacrifice which
rendered her doctrines less difficult of interpre-
tation by the instructed. She has ceased to preach,
even with the dying embers of conviction, that a man
may gain the whole world and yet lose his soul alive.

A responsibility hardly to be exceeded by that of
aristocracy rests upon the leaders of Labour. Every
voice raised to encourage the economic delusions of
Socialism is a voice on the side of vulgarity and
irreligion. Most of the leaders of Labour know perfectly well that economic Socialism is impossible, but
by not saying so with honest courage they commit a
grave sin, a sin not only against society but against
God. For democracy in England, once the most sensible and kind-hearted democracy in Europe, is placing
its faith more and more in the power of wages to buy
happiness, turning away with more and more impati-
ence from the divine truth that the Kingdom of Heaven
is within us.

It is a grievous thing to corrupt the mind of the
simple. Democracy in England has been the chief
representative of veritable Englishness up to these
days. It was never Latinized or Frenchified. The
cottage garden refused to follow the bad example of the
"carpet-bedder." The poor have always been racy
of the soil. They have laughed at the absurdities of
fashion and seen through the pretensions of wealth.

They have believed in heartiness and cheerfulness. All their proverbs spring out of a keen sense of virtue. All their games are of a manly character. To materialize this glorious people, to commercialize and mammonize it, to make it think of economics instead of life, to make it bitter, discontented, and tyrannous, this is to strike at the very heart of England.

But though the leaders of Labour are guilty of this corruption, there is no doubt that the ugliness of spirit in democracy is the reflection of the ugly life led by the privileged classes. There is no reproach for this democracy when it looks upward. It sees nothing but the reckless and useless display of wealth, nothing in the full sunshine of prosperity but a Bacchanalian horde of irresponsible sensualists, nothing there but a ramp of unashamed hedonism, and a hedonism of the lowest order.

Democracy, nursing what it deems to be its economic wrongs, and not unnaturally regarding the wealthy classes with bitter anger, has yet to learn that capital was largely the creation of the Puritan character, and that the prosperity of these British Islands was laid in no small measure by the thrift and temperance of those who lived simply because they thought deeply. Capital, without which Labour could have done little, is not a contrivance of the noisy rich, but the deliberate creation of virtuous men. Capital, now regarded as an enemy, was once the visible best friend of Labour.

Where is there now among the possessing classes an example even of simplicity in dress, modesty in

behaviour, temperance in conduct, and thrift in living?
As for any higher example—an example of wisdom,
duty, self-sacrifice, and moral earnestness—it is nowhere
visible in our national life to those who look upward.

Until we recover this ancient spirit our politics must
continue their descent to the abyss, and democracy
will listen to the corrupting delusions of the economic
Socialist.

We need the Puritan element in our characters, the
Hellenic element in our minds, and the Christian
element in our souls. We must set a higher value on
moral qualities, on intellectual qualities, and on Christian qualities. We must learn to see, not gloomily and
heavily, but with joy and thanksgiving, that our world
is set in the midst of an infinite universe, that it has a
purpose in the scheme of things, that we are all members
one of another, and that there is no grandeur of character, mind, or soul which can ever be worthy of
creation's purpose.

Less flippancy in the world would lead to more serious-
ness, more seriousness would lead to greater intelligence,
and greater intelligence would lead to nobler living.

"The cure for us," said George Sand, "is far more
simple than we will believe. All the better natures
amongst us see it and feel it. It is a good direction
given by ourselves to our hearts and consciences."

Let each man ask himself, Is my direction worthy of
man's past and hopeful for his future?